ON ASSIGNMENT:
the stories behind the stories

INSPIRING EXPERIENCES FROM
AN LDS BROADCAST JOURNALIST

ART RASCON

Covenant Communications, Inc.

*A fireside based on this book
is available on cassette:*

On Assignment: The Stories Behind the Stories

Interior pen and ink illustrations by Kristine Mackessy-Etzel

Published by Covenant Communications, Inc.
American Fork, Utah

Printed in the United States of America
First Printing: August 1998

04 03 02 01 00 99 98 97   10 9 8 7 6 5 4 3 2 1

ISBN 1-57734-294-1

Library of Congress Cataloging-in-Publication Data

Rascon, Art.
     On assignment : the stories behind the stories : inspiring experiences of an LDS broadcast
journalist / Art Rascon.
        p.   cm.
     ISBN 1-57734-294-1
     1. Rascon, Art. 2. Television journalists--United States--Biography. 3. Radio journalists--United
States--Biography 4. Mormons--United States--Biography 5. Church of Jesus Christ of Latter-Day
Saints--Biography.   I. Title.
     BX8695.R37A3 1998
     070'.92--dc21   98-28168
        [b]   CIP

ACKNOWLEDGMENTS

To my lovely wife and best friend, Patti. Her devotion, patience, love, and delicate nudging compelled me to finish this work.

To my five children. Their love and smiles have brought peace and happiness to my life. To my good parents. Their kind words and never-ending support make them unsung heroes.

To my many college instructors and work associates over the years. They have taught me much about journalism and have played an influential role in my life.

And to my dear friends and those I've come to know through coverage of events. They know who they are. Without them, life would be without stories.

CONTENTS

PREFACE

During my career as a broadcast journalist, I have interviewed literally thousands of people in various places around the world. Some have been rich and famous, others poor and desperate. I've met and spoken with everyone from the raging dictator to the reasoning dispassionate; from the proud elitist to the humble emigrant; from the faithful, God-fearing soul to the seemingly faithless wanderer. I have interviewed some of the nation's most notorious killers, debated with the country's top political leaders, and been enlightened by some of the world's most simple-minded people. It has been a most rewarding experience.

The people I have met walk a variety of roads in life; they are part of what makes this world such an interesting weave of the good, the bad, the ugly, and the inspiring. Although the interviews have taught me much over the years, I am sorry to admit that I have forgotten most of them. Some, of course, are more memorable than others—and a few are embedded in my mind like stamped cement. I remember them as if they occurred yesterday.

One such interview was with Elder Henry B. Eyring, an Apostle of The Church of Jesus Christ of Latter-day Saints. I had the pleasure of meeting with Elder Eyring in the winter of 1996, while I was working on a story about the growing phenomenon of religion on the Internet, and how religious organizations were using cyberspace to spread their message abroad. I had previously met with leading members of other denominations, and I felt that a perspective from the LDS point of view would add an interesting element to the story.

I visited with Elder Eyring for nearly an hour prior to our on-camera interview. During our discussion, he reminded me of something I had heard many times from various Christian groups: that I was working for an industry which, by and large, had a negative influence upon the whole of society. "The media," he said, "with its books, magazines, radio, and television, is one of the adversary's most powerful tools of spiritual destruction." He went on to say that men, women, adolescents, and children are being swept away into evil paths, forsaking the principles of Godliness for the momentary pleasure they believe the media, in its own sleazy way, often provides.

I couldn't argue with his observation. I have worked directly with television and radio media for more than fifteen years. I know of its pervasive and negative influence on the lives of millions of people, and I also recognize the shoddy, degrading, and pornographic uses of the print media in the name of profit. There is no question that these are some of Satan's greatest weapons, and he is using them to persuade individuals to turn their hearts away from God.

What impressed me most about my discussion with Elder Eyring is what he said *after* his characterization of the media. "Despite the media's degrading values, we must remember something," he pointed out. "The media is also the Lord's tool of bringing good into the world. We must utilize that purpose, and it's partly your responsibility to make that happen. The Lord has placed you in a position of influence for a reason," he emphasized.

After our lengthy and enlightening discussion, this Apostle of the Lord, looking rather sublime, concluded the conversation in a memorable prophetic tone. "I believe," he said, "that the two greatest influences for good in the lives of the children of men in the next century will be in the fields of communication and education."

His words hit me like a stone to the head, or to the heart. They really pierced my soul. It was one of those moments I look back upon often, knowing his words were meant for me. I realized then, and understand more fully now, the great need to do more.

So, armed with this prophetic charge and challenge to be an "influence for good," I opened my laptop computer and began typing. This book may be a feeble attempt and only a small step toward fulfilling such an admonition. But if even one soul benefits from such a work as this, I will consider the endless hours spent on this project, and away from my family, to be justified.

Since my days of spinning records as a radio disc jockey in Rexburg, Idaho, in 1980, I have worked for nearly a dozen radio and television stations, lived in several cities, and covered events as a reporter throughout the United States and the world. I take no credit for these opportunities and accomplishments; let us give credit where it is rightly deserved and due. The Lord has been the provider of such wonderful experiences and the means of such accomplishments. He has blessed my wife and me with the inspiration necessary to guide our lives and those of our children, and he deserves the deepest admiration, appreciation, and recognition for his abundant outpouring of blessings. I would be guilty of ingratitude if I did not acknowledge the Lord in all things. He has granted me life, talents, the gospel, my family, and indeed, all that I have.

Over the years, the Lord has also blessed me with opportunities to serve in various capacities in the Church, where I have always felt I learned more than I ever gave in return. Many of the callings have involved working with the Young Men's organization of the Church. My greatest joy, outside of my own family, has been serving the youth of the Church. They are the heart and soul of the Lord's latter-day work. During these years, I've had several memorable experiences, some of which I have felt impressed to share in this book. I hope the stories inspire you as much as they have helped and uplifted me.

The stories dealing with my professional career as a news correspondent were much harder to choose. I took a deep, thorough, and time-consuming look at my journal entries, and after a great deal of thought and prayer made my decisions. They were not easy choices.

On the domestic front, I have witnessed the tragic scene of the bombing of the Federal Building in Oklahoma City, and watched as mothers and children lost their lives in the burning of the David Koresh/Camp Davidian Compound in Waco, Texas. I've stood by in stunned disbelief as deadly racial rioting and anarchy swept through the streets of Los Angeles, and I've sat in courtrooms covering some of the country's most notorious trials. In the realm of natural disasters, I've seen the deadly fury of hurricanes, tornadoes, and earthquakes destroy people's lives and property.

Internationally, I have been thrown into the midst of furious border conflicts in Central America. I've stood in makeshift morgues in banana republics, watching helplessly as dozens of people are carried away on stretchers. I've seen the power of evil as it rules countries and terrorizes innocent victims of repression and hate. And in countries struggling to find democracy, I've watched in horror as men were beaten in the streets while throngs of people cheered the attackers. In lands oppressed by communism, I've sat with starving refugees caged in barbed-wire fences, yearning for freedom. Their only spark of hope was a crude drawing of an American flag clutched in their hands.

These are the tragedies and struggles of life, where death, despair, and despondence loom large in the hearts of victims and their families—where all, it seems, is lost, and there is nothing more to live for. But it is also under these troubling and difficult circumstances where heroes are born; where real-life battles are won; where stories of faith, love, and devotion come alive. And where hope lives on.

What I have come to realize, as I cover events throughout the world, is the desperate state of so many people. Confusion, ignorance, speculation, and spiritual blindness run rampant in today's society. So many individuals unknowingly live in bondage, shackled by the chains of sin, unaware of the truth that could set them free and place their feet firmly on a path toward God. As I learn more of the world, the Lord's promise echoes ever louder: "Ye shall know the truth, and the truth shall make you free" (John 8:32).

The common thread in these stories is simply this: By seeking guidance from above, and by following divinely restored gospel principles, we can be a happier people. The great prophet Alma reminded his son, Helaman, of this when he observed, "[God] said: If ye will keep my commandments ye shall prosper in the land" (Alma 37:13). He concluded his counsel with a few simple but profound words which, if followed, would bring more true happiness than any worldly achievement: "Look to God and live" (Alma 37:47). This wise counsel is just as meaningful today as it was in Helaman's time, and its application could literally change the world. As you read the stories on these pages, it is my hope that you will see the wisdom in Alma's prophetic declaration, and renew your own personal determination to "look to God and live."

PART ONE

"LOOK TO GOD AND LIVE"

There is but one absolute truth in this world, and it comes from God. Should we not then look to him in all that we do?

"LOOK TO GOD AND LIVE"

I can vividly recall the first real experience that allowed me to reach beyond the security of my parents' testimonies and truly "look to God and live." I must have been twelve or thirteen years old. Unfortunately, I wasn't keeping a journal at the time, so I'm not certain of my age. But I can vividly remember the surroundings and circumstances that led to a spiritual reformation in my life, accompanied by a deeply rooted testimony of the restored gospel of Jesus Christ.

As you will come to learn in subsequent stories, my adolescent years were not the most memorable or rewarding years of my life. Like all young men, I was experiencing many changes in my life—physically, mentally, and spiritually. Because of this, I frequently felt awkward and out of place. Not only was I trying to discover who I was, but I never had many friends to lean on or confide in during these young years. I was described by many as a loner who spent a great deal more time working various jobs at nearby restaurants than becoming involved in social or sporting events.

During this time, as I contemplated my existence, I began searching for answers and direction. Sure, I understood the lessons from various Primary teachers and Young Men instructors; I was not completely ignorant of the basic fundamentals of the gospel. But deep within me was the burning desire to learn for myself about the existence of God and his Son, and to gain a testimony of the gospel for myself.

I prayed and I read; I pondered and I searched. I attended church and most youth activities regularly. I didn't read as much as I should have, but I made the attempt. My evenings were usually busy with various work responsibilities at home and elsewhere. Although I felt my efforts to find the truth were less than valiant, I was genuinely sincere and earnest in my search, and I subsequently received the answer for which I had been patiently waiting. It was during one of the Church's televised sessions of General Conference.

I can vividly recall my parents and a few of my brothers and sisters gathered around the television set, watching a session of Conference. I was leaning against a center archway near the kitchen, occasionally glancing over at the television screen, when I noticed President Spencer W. Kimball approach the pulpit. I casually listened to his opening remarks, becoming more and more interested in what he had to say with each word that fell from his lips. I don't remember everything he said, but I will never forget the impressions I received toward the end of his remarks.

As this small and frail elderly man bore his witness of the Lord, chills ran up and down my spine and I started to tremble. The feeling was unmistakable. It was clear in my mind that the Spirit of the Lord was touching my heart and soul and trying to teach me the truth about this man. As I listened, my body grew weak and I leaned more heavily against the pillar, slowly lowering myself down into a sitting position. I watched and listened more intently. In his soft but bold manner, President Kimball spoke of his love for the Savior, and his great love of the restored gospel. Each word seemed to hit me to the heart, each sentence ringing truth to my ears. Tears soon filled my eyes, and I can most vividly recall telling myself in a muted voice, but through the clear prompting of the Spirit, "This man really is a prophet of God! He really is the Lord's true prophet!"

I knew what I had said was the truth, for the Spirit had opened my mouth and given me utterance. I had no doubt about it, and I felt as though I wasn't able to prevent the words from coming. There seemed to be real power in what I spoke. The spiritual moment was simply too intense for my physical body; I didn't understand why at the time, but I felt extremely weak and was overcome with emotion. I began to cry. I couldn't believe it! "Why am I crying?" I asked myself. I was too young and embarrassed to think it through, so I hid my face and walked out of the room.

This was my first memorable experience with things of a spiritual nature, and it has become a real cornerstone of my testimony of the restored gospel. It was truly a turning point in my life, instilling within me a greater desire to follow Alma's counsel and "look to God and live." Although I had my frailties and struggled in many ways through adolescence, because of this early experience, I always knew where truth could be found. The spiritual confirmation I had received was the solid foundation I was searching for: the absolute truth about the Lord's living prophet, revealed to me through the gentle whisperings of the Spirit.

One of my favorite scriptural passages, and one which has continually offered me encouragement over the years, is the very title of this section: "Look to God and live." This scriptural mandate comes at the end of two chapters of blessing and counsel given by the prophet Alma to his son, Helaman (see Alma 36 and 37). The guidance, instruction, and promises found within these chapters are some of the most beautiful and inspiring verses of scripture in sacred writ. Alma's admonitions to "trust in God," to "learn wisdom in thy youth," to be "meek, humble, lowly in heart," and to "never be weary of good works," are all words to live by. Is there more significant advice that could be of such tremendous worth in our day? I think not.

All the Lord's teachings can be wonderfully and eloquently summarized in five simple words. "Look to God and live," Alma declared! Therein lies one of the greatest prophetic commands ever uttered. How much better the world would be if this edict was followed.

Each story I have chosen for this section is in some way related to the vital, illuminating concept of looking toward God to find truth, meaning, and hope in our lives.

THE TRUE SAVIOR
Deception in Nicaragua

A few years ago I was in Central America, surrounded by literally tens of thousands of people, all chanting, cheering, and waving flags. It was a massive political gathering during the pinnacle of the campaign for president of Nicaragua. I was standing near the central plaza in downtown Managua while the crowd, which was estimated at close to 100,000, impatiently waited for their hero. They sang songs, paraded banners, danced, and carried on in a riotous way. Finally, two hours behind schedule, their political "savior" emerged from a vehicle. The crowds pushed forward, trying to catch a glimpse of the man, violently lunging toward him, while bodyguards with American-issued M-16 machine guns tried to push the crowds back.

"Let me just touch him," a woman screamed as she was nearly trampled underfoot. She was not the only spectator asking for such a privilege. It seemed everyone wanted to behold this man.

"Help me get closer!" another woman yelled. "I need to get closer!"

During the madness a voice was faintly heard over the loudspeakers, but the crush of people and noise was too great to make out what the voice was saying. It was heard again and again, but was not understood until the multitude quieted down enough to listen to the words.

"People of Nicaragua!" the loudspeaker blared. "People of Nicaragua! Here is the man you've been waiting for! Here is the man who will save this country!" There was a dramatic pause. "Here is Daniel Ortega!"

A thunderous applause followed the announcement. The name seemed to pierce every soul with renewed excitement. It was the name and face the crowd was waiting for. With all eyes now cast toward the front platform, Daniel Ortega fought his way through the mass of people and stepped up to the podium, which was set

high on a large metal riser. It was dark outside, and Ortega was barely visible until the spotlights suddenly turned in his direction. He was dressed in pure white from head to toe, symbolic of his self-proclaimed title as "savior of Nicaragua."

The bright lights and his radiant white attire gave the man what he was looking for: an immortal appearance. He slowly stretched forth both hands, first forward then high in the air, clasping a handkerchief in one hand and waving it from side to side. The multitude went wild, cheering him on more loudly and with increased fervor. I was barely able to make out the screams of some women nearby. "He is an angel! Look at him. Doesn't he look like an angel?"

"Yes! Yes!" someone else yelled.

Meanwhile, mingled among the tens of thousands of rallying people were hundreds of men carrying large boxes filled with bread. They tossed the bread to the hungry souls, who applauded and shouted with appreciation.

As I stood on a raised metal platform overlooking this awesome spectacle, I said silently to myself, *There is something terribly wrong with this picture. This man is treated like a god. I don't believe I've ever witnessed such admiration and awe for an individual.*

Who is Daniel Ortega? He is the unscrupulous dictator who once led this country into the bloodiest civil war in Central American history, and who is largely responsible for the deaths of tens of thousands of Nicaraguans. He was the leader of the Sandinista regime which brutally took control of the Nicaraguan government nearly two decades ago, and ruled the country with an iron fist, arming boys as young as ten with machine guns to fight off the growing number of Contra rebels, the CIA-backed freedom fighters. Ortega eventually relinquished his power to democratic control, then shocked the world by returning in 1996 to run for president. This was the reason I was in Nicaragua—to cover this man whose charisma and magnetism was powerful enough to influence hundreds of thousands of followers, despite his bloody history.

After spending nearly twenty minutes calming the throngs of people, the Spanish orator spoke in his familiar charming fashion. "My brothers, my sisters. The Sandinista Party is back!" The crowds cheered his every word while waving black and red bandannas, flags, and banners. He continued, stealing a phrase once uttered by President George Bush. "I am the new Sandinista—the kinder, gentler Sandinista." Then, with a more subdued delivery, he offered a bit of penitence. "I have done wrong in the past. I am not the dictator I used to be. This is the new Daniel Ortega! The savior of Nicaragua!" The riotous crowd broke out in cheers again.

It was simply amazing. I felt like I was watching a whole nation hang on every word of a beloved king or prophet. But instead, it was a man many might call a "wolf in sheep's clothing," with throngs of people literally throwing themselves at his feet. In this desperate land, where resources are limited, any promise of a better future is a sure bet toward gaining notoriety and acceptance, even if you're a scourge from the past.

What astonished me most about this event was not so much the tremendous number of followers this former hated enemy had, but their gullibility and adulation of him as the "savior of Nicaragua." It was said that Daniel Ortega would bring economic salvation to this impoverished land; he held the answers, supporters said, to everything that was truly important. He sold himself as the "great white god" returning to Latin America, reviving hope and prosperity, and peasants everywhere believed him. Their hopes, faith, prayers, and complete submission were behind this man who symbolically adorned himself in white, and in blatant sacrilege told the thundering crowds that he was "a changed man, reborn and reformed."

Soon enough, Ortega finished his remarks and left the Plaza, taking his bread baskets with him. But still wandering with many unanswered questions were tens of thousands of souls, desperately searching for political and economic salvation. We climbed into our four-wheel-drive vehicle and bullied our way through the thick throng of onlookers, honking our horn for passage the entire way. I shouted through the window in Spanish to those we were passing. "Who would like to sell a Sandinista banner?" I yelled.

I always try to return to my Miami office with some relic that reminds me of the story I'm covering. It took several attempts, but I was finally able to purchase a large black and red Sandinista flag from an Ortega follower. No one, it seemed, wanted to part with their coveted memento of this grand political event. Doing so was considered blasphemy or turning your back on Mr. Ortega. The person who sold me the flag was immediately scorned and ridiculed.

It took us a while, but we finally made it back to our small hotel. By the time we arrived it was well past midnight, and I was worn and tired from several long days spent traversing Nicaragua, catching up with presidential candidates, interviewing them and their subjects, and gathering enough video to give my story the warranted flavor of chaotic confusion that makes up politics in this Central American country.

I was still a bit startled by the mesmerizing conclusion of this evening, but more than ready to call it a night. I offered my prayers and jumped into bed. As I tried drifting off to sleep, I felt a prompting of the Spirit calling me to get up and read the Book of Mormon. It was a burning sensation that I couldn't ignore, so in the dark of night I reached over and flipped the light switch. I grabbed the Book of Mormon, and without any effort on my part, the book fell open to 3 Nephi, chapter 11. I began reading.

"And now it came to pass that there were a great multitude gathered together, of the people of Nephi, round about the temple which was in the land Bountiful..."

My thoughts raced back to the huge, largely Lamanite multitude gathered in the central plaza. It could have been much like the crowd of people in the land of Bountiful. I read on.

"And it came to pass that while they were thus conversing one with another, they heard a voice as if it came out of heaven; and they cast their eyes round about, for they understood not the voice which they heard; and it was not a harsh voice, neither was it a loud voice..."

I was envisioning the throng of people I had been with only hours earlier, all "conversing one with another" and "casting their eyes round about, for they understood not the voice which they heard." I began to see similarities between the two events. I continued.

"...nevertheless, and notwithstanding it being a small voice, it did pierce them that did hear to the center, insomuch that there was no part of their frame that it did not cause to quake; yea, it did pierce them to the very soul, and did cause their hearts to burn."

I remembered witnessing the crowd's reaction after the announcement was made of Ortega's imminent arrival. The similarity of the events was so startling, and yet so very, very different. The scriptures spoke truth to me, while this evening's event portrayed nothing but deception. I read on, realizing with each verse the real miracle of the Savior's appearance.

"And behold, the third time they did understand the voice which they heard; and it said unto them:

"Behold my Beloved Son, in whom I am well pleased, in whom I have glorified my name—hear ye him.

"And it came to pass, as they understood they cast their eyes up again towards heaven; and behold, they saw a Man descending out of

heaven; and he was clothed in a white robe; and he came down and stood in the midst of them; and the eyes of the whole multitude were turned upon him, and they durst not open their mouths, even one to another, and wist not what it meant, for they thought it was an angel that had appeared unto them."

At this point, I began to understand why the Lord directed me to read these verses. The warning to beware of false saviors was clear; for what distinguished the remarkable similarities of the two events was the obvious contrast of truths between them. The Lord's visit to the Nephites was undoubtedly and undeniably true, while this modern-day, self-fashioned messiah was a facade, a big lie, a cunning spectacle. As I read the next several verses of scripture, the beauty and peace of the Lord's spirit filled that small hotel room.

"And it came to pass that he stretched forth his hand and spake unto the people, saying:

"Behold, I am Jesus Christ, whom the prophets testified shall come into the world.

"And behold, I am the light and the life of the world; and I have drunk out of that bitter cup which the Father hath given me, and have glorified the Father in taking upon me the sins of the world, in the which I have suffered the will of the Father in all things from the beginning."

There was great power in these sacred words. A sweet peace filled my being, and I was overcome with a feeling of awe and humility at the Lord's visit and love for the people in the new world. I had read these verses describing the Lord's visit to the Americas many, many times, but I had never felt such truth in them. The Lord's pronouncement through the whisperings of the Spirit was so real and special that evening that I actually felt like one of the inhabitants of the ancient Americas, proclaiming that "There was no part of MY frame that it did not cause to quake; yea, it did pierce ME to the very soul, and did cause MY heart to burn."

I wiped the tears from my eyes and continued to read the stirring record of the Lord's visit. One cannot describe the account more beautifully and poetically than what is already found in holy writ. It is perfect. The majesty and sublimity of it all overwhelms me and reaches my inner emotions. Is it any wonder the Lord directed me to read such scriptural passages on this night of such similarities, yet such deception?

In these Latin American countries, where so much of the Book of Mormon comes to life, the Lord's visit to his people is of paramount significance. It is the grand fulfillment of biblical and new world prophecies bearing record that the Book of Mormon is truly "another testament of Jesus Christ." The book is a divine resource where questions, concerns, and difficulties can be truthfully answered, and where people wandering in today's age of confusion can find a sense of direction.

This evening's remarkable experience only strengthened my testimony concerning the source of absolute truth. It doesn't masquerade itself in a pompous show of lights, spectacles, and theatrics. It is found in the simple but profound words of ancient and modern prophets of God who humbly and meekly seek the guidance of the Holy Spirit to write and speak the words of the Lord. Should we not show the same meekness by learning from them and their works? In doing so, we can become great ambassadors of truth, rising above the "cunning craftiness" of men.

Like all false messiahs, Daniel Ortega eventually lost the election, and indirectly, so did hundreds of thousands of his followers. If we are to "look to God and live," then we must understand that there is no lasting happiness following after anyone other than the Lord Jesus Christ, the true Savior and Redeemer of the world.

SEEKING NEW HOPE
"Welcome to Camp 9"

Some of the most difficult stories I have covered involve the suffering of children who are hungry or cold, abused or forgotten. So many of these little ones are injured, dying or lost, and through no fault of their own, innocently suffer through life in sad, pitiful conditions, usually the direct result of a political system gone awry, the deliberate neglect of parents, or the events of natural disaster.

In my various travels as a correspondent, I am often sent to countries that are not the most desirable places to visit or live. These are countries where extreme poverty, political chaos and ruthless, bloody violence stretch across the land; where desperate people take desperate measures to satisfy their selfish, covetous desires; and where greedy, power-hungry leaders oppress their people. Unfortunately, these areas are usually where the most blatant examples of child neglect and suffering are found. In the Western Hemisphere, there are two such countries that fit this description perfectly. They are the lands of Haiti and Cuba.

Haiti is by far the poorest, and one of the most troubled countries in the Western Hemisphere, where a history of political turmoil has created frequent periods of confusion and anarchy. Brutal dictatorships have been violently overthrown by ruthless militant groups no better than their predecessors, and the lust for power has bathed the country in blood. The heavily armed military rule has kept Haiti isolated from free enterprise, investment, or self initiative. It is a country perceived by many as slowly dying.

I have had the unsavory "opportunity" of traveling to Haiti on a number of occasions. Unfortunately, my visits were during times of political crisis and bloodshed, when men, women, and children were beaten in the streets while crowds stood by and cheered. Even the basic necessities of life are hard to come by here; food, shelter, and drinking water exist, but are by no means plentiful. Most of these necessities of survival are scrounged on the streets, in sewers, and under stripped trees for shelter. It's a sad, pathetic land.

Cuba, of course, is the last holdout of Communism in the Western Hemisphere, still ruled by Fidel Castro, an unyielding dictator, doggedly persistent about his self-proclaimed superiority. He rules his country with a heavy hand and uses the long arm of the law to suppress even the most casual hint of criticism. Communism has ruined this country; it has become a victim of its own politics, a land of never-ending bondage at the mercy of a power-hungry government.

Even so, within these two countries, however corrupt their leaders, are kind, loving people who are hopeful and have a deep, abiding faith in God. They patiently pray for peace, economic rescue, and even freedom. Many of them, desperate to change their circumstances, secretly abandon their homeland in search of a better life. For Cubans, that "better life" is only ninety miles north across the Florida Straits in the Atlantic. For Haitians, it is a much tougher journey—a dangerous 500-mile expedition that has resulted in the deaths of hundreds, possibly thousands of people.

In the summer months of 1994, there was a refugee crisis like no other in the Caribbean, and it literally involved tens of thousands of Cubans and Haitians. During this period, thousands of makeshift rafts and boats drifted to the southern coast of Florida, all carrying freedom-hungry refugees who were starving for a land of hope, opportunity, and religious freedom. Can you blame the courageous who attempted to flee? Considering the alternative, it's no great wonder that so many turned their backs on their countries. What they could not find in their own lands, they knew they could find in the United States.

The following story is just one of many that came out of this refugee crisis. I have chosen to share it because it involved the hope and faith of the future—the children.

"Welcome to Camp 9"

"Take me home with you."

I remember hearing that soft cry from an eleven-year-old boy as he peered through a chain-link fence when I walked by. He looked thin, frail, and had a noticeably sad countenance. His voice echoed with a heartfelt plea of desperation. He was shoeless and shirtless, his hair matted and unwashed, and he wore only an over-sized pair of worn, dirty nylon shorts. I was barely able to make out the unraveling Nike symbol on the left leg, no doubt part of a shipment of donated clothes from the United States.

This boy was not alone. He was surrounded by a dozen or so young Haitian friends in very similar conditions. And not far away, in an entirely separate camp, standing under the blazing sun of the Caribbean, were thousands of Cubans—men, women, and children, all wandering aimlessly. Their home for the past several months had been a large caged detention facility in the middle of a dusty wasteland on the southeast tip of Cuba, at a small American military base known as Guantanamo Bay. This is where refugees from Cuba and Haiti were taken after being caught at sea in their rickety old boats while attempting to cross the wild Atlantic.

The really lucky ones are the thousands who actually made it to the shores of the United States, and are now learning that democracy and capitalism present new struggles that will take some time getting used to.

Then there are the thousands of refugees who never made it much farther than their own coasts. The simple, crude boats they overloaded with human baggage were far from seaworthy, even in a mild storm. The boats and their desperate passengers are forever lost somewhere in the waterways of the Florida Straits or the Great Bahama Bank, both in the Atlantic. We'll never know how many fleeing Cubans and Haitians drowned at sea; records are never kept on the number of boats leaving the islands, and none of the boats ever had a "passenger manifest."

The more than twenty thousand refugees at Guantanamo Bay had some reason to be thankful; at least they were alive, being fed, partly clothed, and given shelter, however archaic it was. Housing consisted of military tents strewn about here and there. And because they were considered illegal immigrants, they were caged in like animals behind barbed wire fences and separated into groups categorized by age, ethnicity, and families. Cubans were placed in a camp on one end of the military base, while Haitians were placed in a separate camp on the opposite end.

The purpose of my visit was to do a story on the Haitian children who had braved the sea without their parents and were now caught in the middle of political squabbling over their future. Would they be allowed to enter the United States, or would fate take them back to their homeland, the miserable country they were so desperate to flee? Washington was deciding the issue even during our trip to Guantanamo Bay. The answer, we knew, would come soon.

As I walked to the Haitian camp and toward an opening of the cordoned-off section of barbed wire, I couldn't help noticing a large sign. "Welcome to Camp 9," it read, as if anyone would be pleased to be there. The words were written on a slab of old, rotted wood, scribbled in an almost unintelligible manner. It was a valiant attempt at hospitality, considering the pitiful, wretched conditions of the camp.

"Camp 9" was a refugee base that housed nearly 300 young men from Haiti. Some were as young as eleven years old, but most were between the ages of fourteen and eighteen. Many of the children came from broken families—fathers who deserted them, mothers who could no longer care for them, and foster parents who no longer wanted them. Others were simply runaways. But no matter what their backgrounds, they all had one common ambition: They were searching for a better life, and they strongly believed God had been leading the way to help provide it.

What made this story so troubling and difficult to cover was that these innocent children desired nothing more than what you or I would righteously seek after: freedom, peace and safety, the necessities of life, opportunity to excel, the ability to accomplish worthy ambitions, and the desire to worship God. They never found this on the ravaged, troubled island of Haiti, but they knew it existed in the United States. Their craving for such a life was the reason they were now in "Camp 9." Relying on promises of what they had heard and seen of the United States, the youth set sail on a several-hundred-mile journey, traveling in groups as small as five and as large as 300, all in boats better fitted for swimming pools than the unpredictable ocean. They left Haiti without their parents, legal guardians, or any adult supervision. Some of the so-called "boats" they traveled on were nothing more than two or three large tires tied together with twine and a slab of plywood on top. Other sea craft they took passage on included larger fishing boats, but none built to handle a five-hundred-mile journey across a rough sea.

Still, with nothing more than visions of new hope, they came. And by the hundreds they were caught and rescued at sea by the United States Coast Guard, usually after some members of the group had already died from severe exposure, lack of food, or disease. Others were sometimes near death, suffering from dehydration, and blistering from exposure to Mother Nature's elements. The Coast Guard was a welcome sight for the refugees; to them it meant food, clothing, shelter, and freedom. Little did they know, however, that they would not be taken to their place of yearning, their land of promise, but instead to a dusty, squalid military refugee camp at the tip of Cuba.

I'll never forget the reaction from those Haitian children as I passed under their "welcome" sign and entered the camp. They rushed upon me like bees on honey, like sugar ants on a piece of crumb cake. The throng of children was so thick around me that I could not move. They reached toward me as if I could save them from their fate, grabbing my pants, legs, arms, and anything else they could get hold of. They tugged on my clothes while shouting in French and Creole, two languages I don't even understand.

Occasionally I heard someone shout in English or even Spanish, two languages I like to think I understand.

"Take me home with you! Take me home with you!" they shouted with wild enthusiasm. Their pleadings were not frivolous attempts at gaining my attention; they were heartfelt pleas to actually bring them home with me. They knew I had come from the land they most desired, and I'm confident they would have been willing to do anything to get there. But did they actually believe I could take them back with me to the United States? They came from a land of little law and order, so to them, it was not an unreasonable request.

Along with the appeals to join me on my return to the States came questions about their fate. They were anxious and hungry to learn any information about what would become of them. I was able to find a few young men who could speak enough English to carry on a conversation. "What will happen to us?" a young fifteen-year-old asked.

"I don't know," I responded. "You may have to return to Haiti, but if they can find homes for you in the United States, you may be able to live there." I know I didn't give them any new information, but I didn't have any to give.

Living in a quandary about the future was hard for these children, and because most had been living in the wretched camp for two or three months, they were eager to leave. Many of the youth had relatives living in Miami who were willing to house them, but the question of whether the United States government would allow it remained unanswered. The Haitian government, not surprisingly, didn't care much about what happened to the children.

My camera crew and I made our way around the camp, gathering the necessary video of their living conditions and speaking periodically with some of the youth. There was one young man who spoke English quite well. His name was Thomas. We followed him to his tent, where about a dozen other young men also lived. Their cramped living quarters were separated by old, stained, donated sheets that hung from the top of the tent. Each small

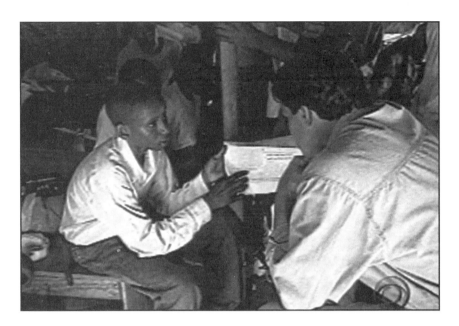

room had enough space for a military cot about two feet wide and five to six feet long. Thomas took us to an open space in the tent where we sat and talked. He told me that his father was dead, and his mother escaped and fled safely to Miami.

You never know what to believe from these children. Most will make up any story that would help get them to the United States. But I believed this story. I could feel the goodness of this young man. "Do you have any other family in Haiti?" I asked.

"My father is dead. They beat him with sticks in the street. I have an uncle and aunt in Haiti, but they don't want me."

I had no reason to doubt the boy. Thousands of people were beaten to death during the political turmoil in that country. I had witnessed some of it. "Why do you want to leave Haiti?" I asked, clearly knowing the answer, but wanting to hear it from this boy.

"I was living with my uncle and older cousin. He has no food. He was beaten, too. I want a better life. I want freedom. I want peace. I want my mama."

Although he shared his tent with several other young men, each small cubicle was personalized in some way. Thomas had several small items pinned to the sheets hanging next to his cot, one of which was a small American flag. He grabbed it with one hand and pointed to it with the other. "I want America!" he said. "I pray every night to go to America. I believe God will take me there." He held his hand high in the air and spoke again. "Red, white, blue. I go to America soon." He stood, and this time he shouted. "I want America! I want America!"

He waved the small flag above his head, and other young men in the tent soon joined in, shouting, jumping, cheering, and grabbing anything they could to bang on. "I want America! I want America! I want America!" they chanted in unison.

As spontaneous as this demonstration was, I couldn't help feeling that they had done it several times before. I'm confident they kept the American soldiers who guarded the camps awake late at night, parading their songs and chants. The banging of pots and pans with spoons and whatever else they could find actually sounded like rehearsed music. It had a nice beat to it. But soon enough, the celebrated optimism came to an abrupt end. Word came from Washington: All Haitian children would have to return to Haiti. All Cuban refugees would eventually be processed and allowed to enter the United States.

Word spread quickly throughout the various camps at Guantanamo Bay. My camera crew and I raced to the Cuban camp to get their reaction, and believe me, it wasn't hard to find. The Cubans, most of them without shoes or shirts, grabbed their makeshift drums and tambourines and began singing an old Cuban victory song. They clapped their hands, waved American flags, and paraded in a large group down the row of tents, causing a dust cloud as they marched, danced, and sang. One man dressed himself in the likeness of Fidel Castro, and in mockery waved to the refugees who openly ridiculed him. It was a true celebration for what was undeniably the greatest moment of their lives. It was what these Cubans had hoped for—to leave a country that nearly four decades ago declared, "There is no God," and to be allowed to live, work, and worship freely in a land they had only dreamt of.

"We go to America!" they shouted. "We go to America!"

On the other side of the military base at the Haitian camp, just a few hundred yards away, a very different scene was unfolding. The sounds were loud cries of anguish and disbelief. All that these children desired had been pulled out from under them, their hopes, dreams, aspirations, and visions of a new life crushed before them. Never before had I witnessed such sorrow and heartbreak. The announcement was a drastic turning point for these children that abruptly took away their lifelong dreams of finding a better life in the land of promise.

"I don't want to go back!" my friend Thomas cried. "I want to go to America!" Other children sobbed with him. Some huddled together for support; others walked off to their small cubicles, trying to hide themselves from what they believed was a vicious, uncaring world. Their faces may have been hidden, but I could hear their cries and sniffles echoing throughout the camp. It was a devastating moment, much too difficult to put into words.

Later that evening, when we had finished gathering our video for the day, I returned to my own camp and tried to get comfortable on my small cot. I couldn't help thinking of the images I had witnessed that day…so many sorrowful and heartbroken souls, and yet so close by, the epitome of celebration. I walked outside of our little shelter and sat with a few American soldiers. Rats the size of rabbits ventured into our little camp, searching for food. Apparently the soldiers I was staying with had trained the rats to come every evening for dinner leftovers. At least the rats were enjoying their time in this desert wasteland.

The United States wasted no time in shuffling the refugees off to their respective locations. The next day, several faded old school buses parked at the entrances to the Cuban and Haitian camps. The refugees were loaded and hauled off to the military base airport, where two large military cargo planes were waiting, separated by perhaps one hundred yards. It was another video-rich, but disturbing scene. The Cubans, in an unrelenting mood of celebration, cheered as they exited the bus and boarded the plane for freedom, while not far away, hundreds of young, heartbroken and teary-eyed Haitian children boarded a plane for their homeland with its frail democracy and uncertain future. I watched as each of the cargo planes took off; one went directly east, toward Haiti, the other northwest, toward the United States. Here, before my eyes, were refugees who knew exactly what they were given, and others who knew exactly what had been taken away. It was the difference between freedom and bondage. The contrast was stark and almost overwhelming.

The next morning I would be returning to Miami, to a country I love and cherish, and leaving behind young Haitian children I can only grieve for. I wondered what would become of these children. Would they return, hungry and helpless, to the streets and slums of Haiti, a country in such chaos that the chance of any of them living past the age of thirty-five was remote at best? This would likely be their future.

I again returned to my camouflage shelter in the middle of this vast, open desert and lay down on that old military cot. Again the rats, that night looking even larger than rabbits, waddled toward us for their near-nightly feeding. I tossed them a few bread chunks and watched as they scurried over and gobbled them up. Boy, were they hungry rats! They were the largest rats I had ever seen.

As I tried to get comfortable, my mind kept drifting back to that scene of refugees boarding the cargo planes. Even today, their faces are embedded in my mind as if the event happened yesterday. Some were filled with laughter, joy beyond measure, and excitement, while others were filled with tears, sadness, and a sense of doom.

Too often, I believe, we take for granted the things we comfortably experience every day. Religious freedom, security, opportunity, and peace are commonplace among those living in free countries, but we can hardly imagine how deeply others yearn for such freedoms and opportunities. The countries of Haiti and Cuba may rank as two of the least desirable places in the Western Hemisphere; yet there are countless people in these countries who genuinely "look to God and live." Many of these refugees, both young and old, carried a deep abiding faith in the Lord and sought his help as they struggled through one of the most difficult periods of their lives. They recognized their pitiful plight and prayerfully asked God for help. Even the young Haitian children, though forced back to their homeland, refused to accept that their immediate fate would be long-lasting. "I will come to America someday," Thomas said as he boarded the plane. "God will take me there someday."

I learned much from these refugees. I realized how often I take for granted even the basic necessities of life—food, clothing, and shelter, not to mention freedom and opportunities. Even the simplest blessings we must not take for granted. On my visit, I took with me dozens of CBS pens and handed them to the throngs of young men who tugged on my clothes. They reached and grabbed for them as if they were twenty-dollar bills. Do we truly recognize our blessings and show appreciation for them? I don't think so; at least I know that I am often guilty of taking many things in life for granted.

Latter-day prophets have told us that ingratitude is one of this generation's greatest sins. I fear that unless we demonstrate heartfelt appreciation for our abundance of blessings as passionately as fifteen-year-old Thomas yearns for them, our ingratitude may be a telling signal of our own doom.

An Interview with CBS News
The Surprising Question

It was March of 1994, and my family was visiting relatives in Orem, Utah. When I called my office in Los Angeles to check my voice mail, there was a message from my agent, Kenny Lindner, who spoke in his usual upbeat tone. "I know you're out of town," he said, "but please call me as soon as you get this message. I have some great news!"

I wondered what it could be. He sounded too excited to just chat about how everything was going. My five-year contract with KABC-TV in Los Angeles was expiring in October of that year, and I knew a search was underway to explore other opportunities at other stations and even the network, but I wasn't anticipating a response so soon. I gave Kenny a call.

"Hey, Art! Guess what?" he said enthusiastically. "How does a job as a network correspondent sound? CBS News called and really, really liked your tape. They would love to see more material."

It was certainly exciting news. I was anxious to make the jump from a local news reporter and anchor to national or international correspondent, and the early interest in my work was encouraging. I told Kenny I would return to Los Angeles, gather more segments of my reporting and anchoring, and have them delivered to his Los Angeles office.

Agents are almost a necessity in this business when trying to move into the country's top markets, and they are certainly needed to break into the hierarchy of the national network news. Television and radio markets are broken into various sizes, ranked by the number of households in the area. For example, New York is the nation's number one market; Los Angeles is market number two; and Salt Lake City is market 39. There are more than 220 markets in the country, and nearly every journalist is trying to work his or her way to the top. The obvious problem with this business is that there are very few positions to fill in top markets, and far fewer on the network level. Agents work closely with management at these levels and may create the "in" that a journalist is looking for. Once management agrees to look at the tape and resume of a prospective reporter, it's the portfolio of work that sells the journalist, not the agent.

I began my broadcast journalism career in 1981 in Rexburg, Idaho, market size 197. I signed on with Kenny seven years later, in 1988, when working in El Paso, Texas, market size 98. From there, I worked in San Antonio for a couple of years, then Los Angeles for five years. I was hired by CBS News in October of 1994. National network news is not considered a "market," since it has the potential of reaching every household in America.

Ever since I was a senior in high school, one of my greatest ambitions and goals had been to be a network correspondent. So, naturally, this phone call from CBS News was the beginning of all I had ever dreamed of. I eventually returned to Los Angeles, gathered more material, and sent it to CBS News.

A couple of weeks passed, and another call came from Kenny Lindner. "Art, they love your work and want to set up an interview," he said.

I was thrilled. Everything seemed to be falling into place. A date was set for an interview with CBS executives in New York, and I spent some time talking with a couple of other network correspondents to learn more about the interview process. I was told it could be a grueling, lengthy, and often intimidating experience. To brush up on current news events and try to broaden my perspective, I read nearly every major newspaper and magazine in the country. Understanding domestic and international news events is important, but someone who knows how to package those events into a concise, creatively written short script for broadcast is also what network executives search for.

I arrived in New York on a Thursday morning and first met with the network president's secretary, who explained how the day of interviews would proceed. I would first sit down for breakfast in the executive lounge with the president and vice president of CBS News, the executive producers of *The Evening News with Dan Rather*, and show producers of *48 Hours*, *60 Minutes*, *Sunday Morning with Charles Osgood*, *The Weekend Show*, and *CBS This Morning*. The national and foreign news editors, who were largely responsible for all domestic and foreign bureaus, would also be in attendance. After the breakfast question-and-answer period I would have individual interviews with various news executives, including the president of CBS News, Eric Ober. To say the least, it sounded like a rather intimidating day. I was already looking forward to the flight home.

I was escorted into the private breakfast room, and there introduced myself to the waiting executives. They sat me down at a large, oval-shaped cherry wood table. After shaking hands and exchanging greetings, we were served breakfast. It began in a quiet way, with the silence broken by Mr. Ober. "Art," he said, "it's good to have you here. We wouldn't have asked you to come if we didn't think highly of your work."

I began to feel at ease. Mr. Ober continued, "It's traditional at these breakfast meetings to spend a couple of hours and ask questions about your past experience and your perspective on today's news events."

My easygoing attitude began to give way to a more edgy, nervous feeling. *Two hours of questioning,* I thought. *What could they possibly want to talk about for that long?*

I would find out soon enough. Breakfast was nearly over, and it was obvious that Mr. Ober was anxious to begin the question-and-answer portion of the meeting. One of the privileges of being president of a company is having the right to ask the first question. The room was quiet, with all eyes focused on Mr. Ober, knowing that his questions would set the tone for the day of interviews. He picked up some paperwork, which included my resume, and began to read.

Here I was, near the pinnacle of my career, at clearly one of the most important interviews of my life as a journalist, waiting and wondering as Mr. Ober slowly perused my resumé.

Of all the questions to ask a prospective network correspondent, what would be the biggest one? I thought. A thousand stories I had covered raced through my mind, every major news event of the day was jumbled in my head, and thoughts of journalism's hottest ethical and legal issues were mired in the pit of sludge that I called my brain. I wondered if I would ever be able to think clearly.

Soon, Mr. Ober was prepared to ask his first question. I listened intently, as did everyone else in the room.

"Art," he said, "tell me about your missionary experience for the Mormon Church."

What? I silently asked myself. *This is his question? He wants to talk about the Mormon Church?*

His inquiry startled, even humbled me. Here I am, sitting among top executives of CBS News, prepared to discuss my coverage of some of the nation's most tumultuous events of the past decade; and of all the important issues we could discuss, he asks me about my missionary experience for the Mormon Church! I suddenly realized that all my years of working in this business could not have prepared me to answer such a question; but I knew my simple, deep love for the Savior and his restored gospel could. It was a perfect question, because it cut to the heart of what should be the most significant issue of our lives: the gospel.

"Sure," I said, feeling at ease and filled with a sense of comfort. I went on to explain the purpose of LDS missions, then shared with the executives my experiences of walking door-to-door for several hours a day, having many of them literally slammed in my face and dealing with rejection thousands of times. Mr. Ober and the rest of the group seemed to be interested in what I had to say. When I finished, the president had a natural follow-up question.

"Then why would you want to do something like that?" he asked. "Why did you serve a Mormon mission?"

This was a perfect opportunity. Little did they know they were about to receive a portion of the first LDS missionary discussion. I explained to the group why I took time during the prime of my life to serve a mission, telling them how strongly I believed in what

I was doing nearly thirteen years earlier, how grateful I was for that experience, and how deeply rooted my faith in the Church still was. "It prepared me," I told them, "physically, spiritually, and mentally, for life's challenges, perhaps more than anything else has. I wouldn't have traded the experience for anything."

The questioning soon took a very different direction and lasted for some time. The rest of the day was then spent talking with the various executives individually. The final one-on-one interview was with the president of CBS, Mr. Ober. It was a short, positive meeting in which I explained to him my desire to work for CBS. Afterward, as I left his office to catch my flight back to Los Angeles, he firmly shook my hand, wished me well, and said, "I think that Mormon mission prepared you in many ways for a job as a correspondent."

I couldn't believe it, but it was true. My mission experience has been the topic of discussion in various gatherings, but I never thought it would be a part of this one. What a testimony to the impression a Mormon mission has on the minds of others. For most nonmembers of the Church, it's looked upon as the epitome of sacrifice for a young nineteen-year-old man. And indeed, it is a sacrifice; but the blessings of "putting your hand to the plow" are too great to overlook. This is the Lord's kingdom. It has been restored in these latter days, and there is no greater work than to proclaim that "good news" to others. It is incumbent upon every worthy young man to serve a mission for the Lord. It is a commandment, reiterated many times through modern-day apostles and prophets.

I look back quite often on my days as a full-time missionary. Taking into consideration my life's varied experiences, I can say with all truthfulness that it was undoubtedly the most enriching and spiritually rewarding experience of my life. Today, my opportunities to teach and baptize are not nearly so frequent; but whenever they occur, I look back with fondness on those tender years as a young missionary, knowing that without that experience I would likely be a very different person today. I know too many people who regret their decision not to serve a mission, many of whom still suffer the consequences of ignoring such a call to serve. When looking at the eternal nature of our existence, a mission is but a blink in time; yet it will have a profound impact on our eternal inheritance. By serving in this way, we accept fully Alma's great mandate to "look to God and live."

I yearn for the day when my lovely wife and I can serve missions together. What a joy it will be to share the gospel. It is not only a commandment, but a privilege—one by which we can "open the windows of heaven" and allow the Lord to pour out blessings upon us in this life and throughout the eternities.

PART TWO

"IF THOU ENDURE IT WELL..."

True faith and trust in God will conquer all doubts, trials, and afflictions; and in the end bring us closer to God.

"IF THOU ENDURE IT WELL..."

FOREWORD

When it comes to adversity, trials, and afflictions, few endured more than the Prophet Joseph Smith. Like the prophets of old, he suffered every imaginable type of persecution. It began early in his life, only months after his first vision of God the Father and his Son, Jesus Christ. He was scarcely fourteen years old at the time, but the persecution was real, and it continued until the day he gave his life for the restored gospel of our Lord.

Throughout his short life, Joseph was beaten, robbed, forcibly driven from place to place, unjustly imprisoned, mocked, and ridiculed. Everywhere he traveled, he was confronted with violent opposition and near assassination. He was mobbed, deserted, forgotten, and betrayed by many who had once called him "friend." He was forced to live in hiding, hunted at times like a wild animal, all while true friends and members of his own family suffered the pains of mob attacks. Yet, through it all, Joseph was forever devout, patient, and long-suffering; for he had a clear understanding of the existence of God the father and his Son, Jesus Christ. He was their latter-day mouthpiece who would be the instrument of the Restoration during this dispensation of the fullness of times. His faithfulness and endurance were the very reasons he suffered the epitome of personal sacrifice: the loss of life itself, as he sealed his testimony with his own blood.

The Prophet Joseph was not alone in his sufferings. There was rarely a time when the early Saints did not struggle through the pains of deep adversity. They, too, were the focus of ruthless attacks and mob mentality during this ever-changing time of religious fervor. It was a crucial testing period for the Saints. Many left the Church, denied their testimonies, and spoke in open rebellion against the Prophet. Others proved faithful in all things and led the way westward, strengthening others along the way.

Some of the most uplifting passages of latter-day scripture describing these difficult early periods of Church history are found in Doctrine and Covenants 121, 122, and 123. All three sections of prayer and revelation were written and received while Joseph was held prisoner in the jail at Liberty, Missouri, during the winter and spring months of 1839. They are truly some of the most beautiful passages of holy writ.

The Prophet had been unjustly imprisoned for some time in the Liberty jail, while outside the Saints were being mobbed, persecuted, and scattered. It was one of the most distressing periods of the early Church, and Joseph felt helpless. It was during this tremendously painful time that the Prophet, searching for inner peace, began writing. What subsequently evolved was a beautifully inspired prayer, and later, the revealed word of the Lord.

Only portions of the prayer are actually used in these sections of the Doctrine and Covenants, but the Prophet's heartfelt emotion is evident. When all seemed lost, he made a passionate and earnest supplication to the Lord for assistance. He pleaded for relief, for justice against his oppressors, and for peace during a time of great despair. "O God, where art thou?" he wrote. "And where is the pavilion that covereth thy hiding place? How long shall thy hand be stayed, and thine eye, yea thy pure eye, behold from the eternal heavens the wrongs of thy people?

"Yea, O Lord, how long shall they suffer these wrongs and unlawful oppressions, before thine heart shall be softened toward them, and thy bowels be moved with compassion toward them?" (D&C 121:1-3).

In obvious anguish of heart, Joseph continues his written supplication to the Lord: "Remember thy suffering saints, O our God; and thy servants will rejoice in thy name forever" (D&C 121:6).

The Lord answers in his ever constant, loving, compassionate way: "My son, peace be unto thy soul; thine adversity and thine afflictions shall be but a small moment;

"And then, if thou endure it well, God shall exalt thee on high; thou shalt triumph over all thy foes" (D&C 121:7-8). In additional words of peace and comfort, the Lord declares, "Know thou, my son, that all these things shall give thee experience, and shall be for thy good" (D&C 122:7).

God's revealed word is one of the most comforting reassurances of the great love he has for his children. The Lord takes notice of all things; he understands our weaknesses and our strengths. He knows our limits, and yet often allows challenges and afflictions to stretch those limits so that we might learn, grow, and be strengthened in the process.

It has often been said that our quality of life depends not so much on how we act, but how we react. Every day, when we are confronted with various decisions, circumstances, and situations, we are forced to react. It's vitally important that our reactions to these daily challenges are guided by the Spirit of the Lord; indeed, it could very well be of eternal consequence. For how can we follow in the footsteps of our Savior unless we do as he would have us do? Live as he would have us live?

Our resolve to be a better, stronger, more faithful and obedient people is tried daily. We are destined to win, however. We *can* overcome. The Lord did not send us to this earth to fail or to have a mediocre inheritance. God, our Father, sent us here and blessed us with the capability of finishing the test, conquering all, and some day joining him in the eternities. We are gods in embryo, going through a refiner's fire, being molded, shaped, and prepared for greater things. Even so, the Lord realizes that not everyone will return to his presence; some will be lost, and others will simply not try hard enough.

It is crucial to remember that the Lord does not present us with challenges that we cannot overcome. Through the Atonement, our Savior has suffered and experienced every trial and affliction we have faced or will ever suffer. During his hours of agony in Gethsemane, he took upon himself the pains, burdens, and afflictions of every living soul from Father Adam to the end of time. The Lord suffered that he might know and understand our misfortunes; but more importantly, he suffered to atone for our many, many sins and imperfections. "… As a lamb to the slaughter" (see Isaiah 53:7; Mosiah 14:7), the Lord died that we might live.

"Though your sins be as scarlet, they shall be as white as snow" (Isaiah 1:18). What a tremendous blessing we are promised if we turn to the Lord and plead for his mercy. Although repentance requires patience and endurance, it can and must be done. The Atonement is given to us freely; our part consists of exercising faith, humbling ourselves, and approaching the Lord with genuine meekness of heart. As we do this, we will be able to apply the scriptures to our own lives, secure in the comforting knowledge that "all these things shall give thee experience, and shall be for thy good."

If we willingly accept the experiences of our lives, even greater blessings will come. A loving Father in Heaven has given each of us the same divine promise that the Prophet Joseph Smith received: "If thou endure it well, God shall exalt thee on high."

TRAGEDY IN THE HEARTLAND
A Terrorists' Bomb in Oklahoma City

The date was April 19, 1995, a beautiful spring morning. It was the Easter season, a time when the Christian world celebrates the resurrection of our Lord, and when America celebrates something of a new beginning; a springtime awakening of life. But instead, on this day the nation was mourning the loss of dozens of its citizens in the worst act of domestic terrorism in this country's history.

The Murrah Federal Building in downtown Oklahoma City was destroyed by a blast that literally caused half the building to collapse, sending dozens to their deaths. The explosion killed 168 people. Lives were lost, families shattered through the hateful actions of others. I was immediately dispatched to Oklahoma City to help in CBS's coverage of the enormous tragedy. I don't mind saying that the story was one of the most difficult events I have covered in my years as a journalist. It was heart-wrenching, painful, and yet in many ways, spiritually uplifting.

I was at the epicenter of the horrific scene, witnessing a nation at its worst, and realizing just how vulnerable we really are. It was a dramatic reminder of how much evil still exists in this land of promise. Even so, while witnessing the dark side of some individuals, I also came face to face with the good in many people and, in doing so, saw a nation at its best. Never before have I seen such love, devotion, and outpouring of concern. It was beautiful. It was touching. It was true America.

I kept a fairly extensive journal record during my time in Oklahoma City, and am including several excerpts in this work. The writing is somewhat ragged (much of it was written in haste, and not really intended for public consumption), but I hope its substance will give you a sense of understanding and proximity to the people and places I describe, as well as an appreciation for some of the uplifting stories behind this tragic event.

4-19-95—Wednesday

I hear on the radio while driving to work that there has been some sort of large blast in Oklahoma City. Said the radio reporter, "This just in, there has been an explosion in Oklahoma City. We're not quite sure what it was. There are no reports of injuries, but reports say it was heard and felt over a large area of the city." By the time I arrived at my office, CNN news was showing pictures of the blast. It looks bad, real bad. The entire Dallas bureau is on its way to Oklahoma City. I've been told to prepare to leave.

4-22-95—Saturday

What a tragedy this is. This is a city in deep grief. Did a story tonight on families waiting for word about loved ones still missing. I witnessed the deep pain and suffering this city is going through. It was painfully difficult to watch, and even more difficult for families to wait.

With tears streaming down his face, a grown man expressed his genuine love for his wife. You see, she is dying. She lies in bed, in a comatose state, with a crushed skull. "If God decides to bring her home, then I'm just thankful for the time that he gave me with her," he said. "But I'm greedy; I would like to keep her a while." Her four children would like to keep her as well. They range in age from 10 to 17. They sit in vigil at the intensive care waiting room. Outside, buried beneath tons of debris, are the bodies of more than 150 people. The digging moves at a desperate pace in hopes someone might be found alive.

4-23-95—Sunday

There was evidence today that, for the most part, America is a God-fearing, God-loving nation. From

New York to California, people mourned. A nation cried. Torn from tragedy in the heartland. The President declared this day a national day of mourning. Bells were tolled, church pews were full, songs were sung. People prayed. It was a day to offer comfort and a day to ask why. Why must so many die?

A woman with tears running down her face sits and listens as her minister makes a frail attempt at comforting her and the congregation. Held tightly to her bosom are two small teddy bears. One for each child she lost. Aaron was only 5 years old, his brother, Elijah, only 2. They will be buried on Wednesday.

Mothers, fathers, sons, daughters, relatives, friends; it seems everyone knew someone involved in this disaster. There was a massive memorial service today. Ten thousand people attended. The opening hymn was "Amazing Grace." Never before have I seen such a multitude of people so moved and filled with the spirit of love, hope, comfort, peace, and tears.

The real tragedy here is beginning to set in. The stories are beginning to hit me emotionally. A fire-fighter rushes to the building, only to learn that his wife is buried in the rubble. A woman, expecting a child, is crushed by the debris. Workers try to save the baby but can't. Her husband takes us to his home and shows us the baby's room, all prepared, ready for the big arrival. Instead of witnessing life born, he will be burying his wife and his unborn child. A terrible loss, just the beginning. The tragedy of loss here is horrifying. It is unbelievable. It will forever change the lives of Americans and how they view their own security. We feel invaded. This type of thing doesn't happen in the United States. This is a sane society, or so we have always believed it was.

Bells welcomed dusk to this somber city. Another day has passed in what has seemingly felt like a never-ending horrifying dream. Tomorrow, when a new day dawns, there will be more tears, more heart-wrenching stories, more funerals and yes, more victims pulled from their concrete graves.

4-24-95—Monday

It is hard for this city to awaken. Many people don't feel the need to. They have lost so much, and it will take time for this city to heal. There is a permanent scar on the heartland. Something like this can never be forgotten. There were more funerals today. More victims pulled from the debris. It is seemingly a never-ending effort to dig out the dead and hopefully find a few living. But so far, none have been found.

4-25-95—Tuesday

At the bomb site again this morning. I slowly walked around the perimeter of the blast. The damage to buildings and homes around the federal building is surprising. A 15-block area of the city has been closed off. What a powerful blast it was, now forever embedded in the minds of hundreds, if not thousands. I witnessed a poignant example of that while walking around the building this morning.

At the foot of a corner street sign, not far from the bomb site, rests a memorial. Loving friends, concerned residents, and bereaved family members have come to this location to pay their respects to the dead … to mourn the loss of so many, and to comfort each other. An American flag hangs proudly from the corner sign. Underneath, there is a bed of flowers, gifts, pictures, and notes, placed by the many visitors. My mind drifted while studying this memorial. Here was the work of loving hearts and hands. The touch of innocence, mingled with the sorrow of death.

As I looked at this hallowed corner, I saw a young boy, no older than 8 years old, slowly approach the makeshift memorial. In one hand he held tightly to a small, beautifully colored flower. In the other, he held tightly to the hand of a woman. He was teary-eyed as he approached. He walked slowly, and the closer he came to the memorial, the more emotional he became. His eyes were focused on the corner memorial. He began to cry. "This little boy must have lost someone dear to him," I thought. How difficult it must be to come to this location and pay respects to those you love. As the boy stopped at the memorial, he wiped his tears with the same hand that held the flower. Looking down at the flowers, he began to openly cry. He let go of the woman's hand and gently fell to his knees, placing his small flower upon the others. While tears were streaming down his face, he clutched his hands together in a reverent fashion and stared at the memorial site. When he finally stood, he turned and

hugged the woman whose hand he was previously holding. "I love you, Mom," he said. "I love you too," his mother replied. Surely this boy has lost his father, his brother, sister, or perhaps some relative, I told myself. His emotion is too great. It was a moment captured in time only by the deep feelings both boy and mother expressed for each other. They hugged, they cried, they spoke of the love they shared for one another.

As they slowly walked away, I approached the young boy. "Excuse me," I said, "What's your name?" After an emotional hesitation, he said, "David." "How old are you?" I asked. "Eight years old," he said. Then, to satisfy my own curiosity after witnessing his deep emotion at the memorial site, I asked, "Did you know someone who was in the federal building?" He started to cry. How could I put this child through more pain, I thought, than to question him about a possible loved one who died in the explosion? He paused, and with a broken, emotional reply gave this startling answer: "I don't know anyone in the building. I'm just sad for all the people who died. I'm just sad for all the children in there. I wish no one would have bombed the building." He turned to his mother and gave her a hug. I put my arm on the boy's shoulder and said, "Thank you for sharing that with me." I walked away. "Thank you," I thought to myself, "for showing me what loving your neighbor really means."

I have witnessed the pain and suffering of those who have lost loved ones, the grief of someone losing a dear friend, the sorrow of a family member losing a brother, sister, father, or mother. But never before have I witnessed such pain, such grief, such love from a child who never knew those he was grieving over. He loved the victims of this tragedy as a mother would love her own children. His heart was so deeply touched that he painfully mourned their loss. What better example have we than this of one who is willing to "...bear one another's burdens,...mourn with those that mourn, comfort those that stand in need of comfort" (Mosiah 18:8-9), and above all, "love thy neighbor" (Mark 12:31)? It was an eight-year-old boy who taught me the greater meaning of these passages—a lesson by example that I will never forget.

4-26-95—*Wednesday*

9:02 a.m. A day of remembrance today. Exactly one week ago at this time, in this otherwise quiet city in the middle of the heartland, the earth shook, windows shattered, and a building tumbled to the ground. In reverence for that moment, at 9:02 a.m. America stopped. Church bells tolled the song "Amazing Grace," then silence. From New York to Los Angeles, business stopped. In schools throughout Oklahoma City and many other cities, children held hands. At the site of the blast, workers rested their shovels and picks and bowed their heads. Traffic along Oklahoma City's busiest expressway came to a halt. One moment later, at 9:03 a.m., America moved again. One moment of silence, locked in time...remembering those who died and the many more still missing.

4-27-95—*Thursday*

I was told I would be staying several more days. I sent flowers to Patti and then told her the news. This has been an emotionally difficult story to cover. This is the most significant domestic story of the decade, perhaps the century. It's upsetting and terribly unfortunate. Terrorism is an ugly reality that America has dealt with for decades, but never this deadly in our own homeland. It is a wake-up call for America. Now

that other fanatics have seen what can be done, and
with relative ease ... I fear it will happen again.

5-1-95—Monday

I'm writing this on a plane, leaving a city in anguish.
Mixed emotions fill my mind. There is, in some small
measure, a desire to stay and suffer with them. A
desire to help. So many people lost so much. It seems
everyone here knew someone in the building. I was at
the site this morning for my last live shot. Once again,
at this early hour, I saw people walking their way
around the perimeter of the federal building ... stop-
ping and staring, awestruck by the deadly magnitude
of the blast. They walk past the makeshift memorial
and pause for their own moment of silence. It is a
grief-stricken town that I leave behind ... and in some
way will carry with me forever.

THE TEMPEST IS RAGING
A Hurricane's Fury

The most destructive hurricane in 1996, and the worst to hit the East Coast since Hurricane Andrew devastated southern Florida, was Hurricane Fran. The eye of the storm passed just north of Wrightsville Beach, North Carolina, in September of that year.

The hurricane carried steady winds of 135 miles per hour, gusts of up to 150 miles per hour, and sea swells of fifteen to twenty feet. The coastal islands of Topsail Beach, Surf City, and North Topsail Beach were literally submerged during the storm. The homes on those islands were buried in the sand, debris, and water; in some cases, only a rooftop was visible. Those who have witnessed a hurricane's fury understand how the raging sea can be a menacing, awesome force of destruction.

Further inland, it was the wind that did the damage. Many structures had nothing left but a skeleton frame. The wind was so powerful that hundreds of trees were stripped of branches and toppled onto power lines, vehicles, and houses. The scattered debris filling the streets and walkways was so thick in many neighborhoods that even rescue vehicles could not maneuver their way through. The debris was literally everywhere.

Nothing went undamaged from this powerful hurricane. Its tremendous force literally cut a swath of destruction a hundred miles long and several miles wide. Fortunately, there were few lives lost in this disaster; but the damage estimates quickly mounted into the billions of dollars.

Covering such tragedies is always difficult. There is so much pain and suffering, and the loss is so great that a sense of hopelessness surrounds the victims. Those who have some semblance of a home have no running water or electricity, and even the basic utilities are usually dysfunctional for days, if not weeks. Ice suddenly becomes a precious commodity, and at times is sold on street corners for ten times its value. Other necessities like chain saws and generators also sell at a premium. If you've ever experienced a natural disaster, you know exactly what I'm talking about. Day-to-day living suddenly becomes an extreme hardship, and the fundamental necessities of life can no longer be taken for granted.

Reporting from the scene of a hurricane is unlike covering any other natural disaster. Tornadoes and earthquakes occur in an instant, with little or no warning, and reporters usually don't arrive until the destruction has already occurred. Hurricanes, on the other hand, can be seen forming hundreds of miles away, giving residents ample time to evacuate and the media plenty of time to position themselves in harm's way; where forecasters predict the storm will hit.

Over the years, I have covered nearly a dozen major hurricanes. During most of the storms, my camera crew and I were positioned on the coast, directly and purposefully near the eye of the storm, where the most fierce and destructive winds circled. It is the bizarre nature of reporters to place themselves in the line of fire while everyone else flees. Perhaps it's part of the thrill and desire to cover a story from where it's actually taking place.

During the coverage of Hurricane Fran, I was once again on the coast, watching the horrific power of nature bear down in a most unyielding, pernicious way. The crew and I were positioned fifty yards from the beach in a leaky, wind-torn hotel. Windows were shattering around us and debris was flying everywhere. After several hours of a torrential downpour and relentless wind gusts, there was an awesome, almost frightening calm. The eye of the storm was upon us, where the surrealistic stillness of the air delivered a false sense of security. It didn't last long. Soon, very soon, the eye passed and the wind began again in earnest, ripping and tearing through structures just as it had before, only this time the incessant pounding came from the opposite direction.

When the hurricane finally diminished in strength and moved farther inland, the real damage became more evident. The barrier islands of North Carolina were literally destroyed. My cameraman

and I flew up and down the coast in a helicopter, inspecting what was left by the storm and taking video for our story. The damage along the coast was catastrophic. Every structure, it seemed, was lost. Homes and businesses farther inland didn't fare much better.

I reported the disaster from North Carolina throughout the week. The stories were endless: people trying to get their torn lives back together, communities struggling to unite and rebuild, families living in shelters with no homes to return to, and the faithless turning to God, seeking answers.

The Sunday morning following the storm was an active church day for most residents of the beachside community I was reporting from. Chapels and pews were nearly filled in every denomination. Many of the buildings suffered extensive damage, but that didn't stop the faithful from attending; I even saw some congregations meeting in parking lots. It seems that during times of prosperity there is an attitude of complacency, whereas during times of turmoil and strife people rush to find comfort in numbers, examining their relationship with God with increased interest. On too many occasions, I have witnessed tragic circumstances bringing people closer to their Creator, often uniting broken communities, neighborhoods, and even families. It is a promising consequence of disaster, however unfortunate its means.

The most vivid memory of my nearly two weeks in North Carolina was on that first Sabbath morning, when I was sitting in a Mormon chapel, listening to the words of a good bishop. I don't cover hurricanes wearing a suit and tie; so, lacking the formal wardrobe, I wore jeans and a khaki shirt to church that morning. I thought perhaps my attire would not be suitable, but after entering the chapel I realized I was in harmony with the rest of the congregation. Nearly everyone on that beautiful, calm fall morning was wearing clothes more suited to doing heavy yard work than attending church.

The bishop, who was wearing Sunday dress, conducted the service. "It's good to see so many at church today," he said. "I'm glad to see you have been busy cleaning. I only hope that you have been helping your neighbors, friends, and fellow Saints, and not just yourselves."

I don't remember the opening hymn at that Sabbath morning church meeting, but I do recall a solemn, emotional mood. All members in attendance were affected in some way by the storm, and this was their first opportunity to gather as one, lifting their voices in reverent prayer and supplication to the same God who had created the wind and the rain. The meeting was a peaceful, yet stirring confirmation of the difficult and troubling lives each of the members now faced.

In hopes of calming their sorrowful hearts, the bishop turned to the Gospel of Mark and read the biblical account of the Lord calming the Sea of Galilee. The writer describes the event this way:

> And when they had sent away the multitude, they took him even as he was in the ship. And there were also with him other little ships.
>
> And there arose a great storm of wind, and the waves beat into the ship, so that it was now full.

And he was in the hinder part of the ship,
asleep on a pillow: and they awake him, and say
unto him, Master, carest thou not that we perish?

And he arose, and rebuked the wind, and said
unto the sea, Peace, be still. And the wind ceased,
and there was a great calm.

And he said unto them, Why are ye so fearful?
How is it that ye have no faith?

And they feared exceedingly, and said one to
another, What manner of man is this, that even the
wind and the sea obey him? (Mark 4:36-41)

We are all faced with challenges in our lives, sudden storms
that can be potentially destructive to our spiritual or physical well-
being. Some storms of life, such as this hurricane, or even serious
sin, are frightening and devastating to an individual's life, and may
even cause one to cry out in anguish, "Master, carest thou not that
we perish?"

There is a familiar hymn that speaks of these storms of life. Its
origin is, of course, the story of the ancient apostles' plea to the
Lord to save them from the raging tempest. The good bishop of
the congregation turned to that hymn, knowing well enough that
it was speaking directly to his troubled flock—and, I might add, to
all of us who are threatened by personal despair, whether it be
through sin or the ravages of natural disaster.

The hymn, "Master, The Tempest Is Raging," was written by
Mary Ann Baker some time after this poor woman lost her parents
and brother to a respiratory disease. Mary's faith and trust in a
loving God greatly diminished after the death of her kin, and she
soon found herself forsaking the Lord. Before long, she realized her
weaknesses and learned that only the God of life and love could
calm the rough winds and waves of her life. When her faith
returned, she wrote of her experiences in poetic verse, an inspiring
tribute to Him who questioned, "Why are ye so fearful? How is it
that ye have no faith?"

Master, the tempest is raging!
The billows are tossing high!
The sky is o'ershadowed with blackness.
No shelter or help is nigh.
Carest thou not that we perish?
How canst thou lie asleep
When each moment so madly is threat'ning
A grave in the angry deep?

The words pierced the hearts of the congregation. You could see the anguish on their faces as the bishop read the first verse of this hymn. Each new sentence brought back horrifying memories of the tempest they had only recently witnessed with their own eyes, and fortunately lived through. I'm sure they must have felt as though the hymn was echoing their very thoughts. The bishop continued with the second verse:

Master, with anguish of spirit
I bow in my grief today.
The depths of my sad heart are troubled.
Oh, waken and save, I pray!
Torrents of sin and of anguish
Sweep o'er my sinking soul,
And I perish! I perish! dear Master.
Oh, hasten and take control.

And the chorus:

The winds and the waves shall obey thy will
Peace, be still.
Whether the wrath of the storm-tossed sea
Or demons or men or whatever it be,
No waters can swallow the ship where lies
The Master of ocean and earth and skies.
They all shall sweetly obey thy will.

Peace, be still, peace, be still.
They all shall sweetly obey thy will.
Peace, peace, be still.

And then the final verse, with comforting, peaceful lyrics that too often go unnoticed. They are the sweet promises of the Lord, and his reassurance that in response to our genuine pleas, he will take control of our ship tossed at sea.

Master, the terror is over
The elements sweetly rest.
Earth's sun in the calm lake is mirrored,
And heaven's within my breast.
Linger, O blessed Redeemer!
Leave me alone no more,
And with joy I shall make the blest harbor
And rest on the blissful shore. (*Hymns of The Church of Jesus Christ of Latter-day Saints* [Salt Lake City: The Church of Jesus Christ of Latter-day Saints, 1985], No. 105.)

There was a sweet stillness when the bishop concluded his reading of the hymn—a moment of pondering, perhaps, that members of the congregation needed. This was a time in their lives when it seemed that the raging waters of hell were crashing in upon them. Many were faced with what may have been the worst and deepest trial of their lives. But no matter how violent, damaging, or destructive their afflictions, trials, or adversities were, they could hold fast to this simple truth: The Lord, who had overcome all, who could easily command the elements on the Sea of Galilee, could also calm the troubled waters of their lives.

Each of us needs to learn this important, comforting truth. If it is sin that weighs heavily on our shoulders, the Lord has called on us to "come unto me, all ye that labor and are heavy laden, and I will give you rest" (Matthew 11:28). Through sincere and genuine repentance, we can place our burdens upon the Lord; and, as promised, if our sorrow is true and unfeigned, he will grant us peace and rest.

The Lord said, "In the world ye shall have tribulation: but be of good cheer; I have overcome the world" (John 16:33). We live in a world filled with adversity and wickedness. Sin knocks at every door and lurks around every corner. One would be naive to think he or she could wander through life without experiencing violent storms, whether they be through natural disaster, the loss of loved ones, physical or financial distress, or the shackles of sin. How we deal with each storm is the more telling part of our faith in the Lord.

Like Mary Ann Baker, our faith may be strained at times. But let us remember the inspired words of this woman's sweet song:

> *Whether the wrath of the storm-tossed sea,*
> *Or demons or men or whatever it be,*
> *No waters can swallow the ship where lies,*
> *The Master of ocean and earth and skies.*
> *They all shall sweetly obey thy will.*
> *Peace, be still, peace, be still.*

150 YEARS LATER
The Modern-Day Mormon Wagon Train

Recently, on the dusty plains of central Nebraska and under the blazing sun of the Midwest, history was made and revisited. The year was 1997, one hundred and fifty years after the forced migration across the central plains of thousands of early pioneers of The Church of Jesus Christ of Latter-day Saints. In an effort to relive that journey, hundreds took part in a one-thousand-mile reenactment of that trek to the Great Salt Lake Valley.

Today, Salt Lake City is a bustling metropolis; but in 1847 it was a desolate land, an uncharted valley that was forsaken by early trappers. In fact, Brigham Young was told many times that the Salt Lake Valley would never support a large population. The prophet knew the doubters were wrong, for he had seen in vision the desert blossoming as a rose; and indeed it has.

With that same vision and zeal to understand what the early pioneers experienced, scores of Latter-day Saints, trail enthusiasts, and history buffs set out on the same rough, wheel-carved trail used by the early pioneers. They even began their westward trek on the same day the early pioneers started their exodus: April 21. Many even tried to make the experience as authentic as possible by sewing homemade dresses, washing clothes by hand, cooking traditional foods of the day, and sleeping in tents.

This trek from Omaha, Nebraska, to Salt Lake City was a three-month journey for wagon train participants, and an opportunity for the LDS Church's Public Communications Department to capture some media exposure. The Church, realizing the visual potential of this event, wisely pushed the story to local and national media outlets.

I recall receiving an impressive information packet and spending time on the phone with LDS public relations workers in New York and Salt Lake City. There was no question in my mind that the reenactment would make a terrific feature story. It had all the elements of a compelling piece: great video, wonderful stories, and a fair amount of substantive historical news.

It wasn't until a visit to CBS headquarters in New York City that I pitched the story as a possible "Window On America" piece. "Window" pieces are stories which generally run four to five minutes on the national *CBS This Morning* program. An insightful article in *Time* about the modern-day pioneer journey supported my pitch that the reenactment was truly a story of national interest.

I made the pitch during a morning meeting with a "Window" producer, and by early afternoon I was given clearance to cover the story. I was thrilled. It would be an opportunity to give an accurate portrayal of an event that forever changed the face of the western United States, and to bring to light the great struggles, sacrifices, and injustices that led to and were part of the Mormon migration.

Our crew met up with the wagon train during the fourth week of its three-month journey. The entourage of wagons, horses, handcarts, and walkers was about ten miles west of North Platte, Nebraska, traveling at a pace of about ten to fifteen miles a day. They would usually reach their daily destination by mid-afternoon.

What impressed me most about this extraordinary group of modern-day pioneers was their zeal to experience what their gospel forbears had lived and died for. They were earnestly trying to go back in time, to 1847, when struggles and hardships had to be faced head-on. This was their opportunity to revisit history and, in a sense, make a little of their own.

One experience on the wagon train touched me so deeply that I felt my mind was opened to a new understanding of the history of our Mormon pioneers. On the second day of our journey, we stopped at what was believed to be the burial site of an unknown child who probably died sometime during the 1850s. The remote location and its beautiful surroundings are as vivid in my mind today as when I was there. There was an open prairie with rolling hills, and to the south of the trail, about 100 yards, was a thick gathering of trees. Nestled at the edge of the trees and the prairie was a stone marker, the burial place of the small child.

I watched closely as nearly 200 participants in the trek, dressed in traditional pioneer clothing, formed a circle around the stone. Weeks of traveling this harsh land had taken their toll on many of the modern-day pioneers; their faces were weathered and sunburned, their outward appearance dusty and worn. But their hearts were meek and submissive, obviously touched by the spirit of the occasion. For several minutes, they stood silently and reverently around this sacred but crude-looking burial site. No words were spoken or abrupt movements made, but I clearly remember their eyes, focused on the stone marker that would, for them, symbolize the tremendous sacrifices of tens of thousands of early Mormon pioneers.

Following a period of silent meditation, a gentleman walked to the center of the circle. "We are here today," he said, "to rededicate this grave of an unknown child." His voice began to break as he tried to finish, "…and to remember the sufferings of the Saints and all the thousands of children and adults who died along this trail." The officiator at this ceremony was a stake president in Nebraska. He was also the chairman of the wagon train, and was so intimately involved in the experience that he truly carried the spirit of the early pioneers. "Before we begin," he said, "let us sing 'Come, Come, Ye Saints.'"

This has long been one of my favorite hymns; it's difficult to sing without envisioning the sufferings of the early Saints. The song epitomizes the hardships, faith, and vision of our gospel forbears, and its message is a testament to the world of their arduous journey. But on this day, it was also a testament of the Lord's great love for his children; for as we sang that stirring hymn in this remote valley of death, where so many innocent, God-fearing men, women, and children lost their lives, hearts were touched and eyes were opened to the struggles of thousands of faithful pioneers.

In unison, and in an effort to muster true pioneer spirit, the crowd began to sing:

> *"Come, come, ye Saints, no toil nor labor fear,*
> *But with joy wend your way.*
> *Though hard to you this journey may appear,*
> *Grace shall be as your day"*

Never before have I heard a congregation of Saints sing with such fervor, with such feeling and emotion. You could see it in their faces; you could hear it in their voices; and you could sense their conviction to the gospel truths so proudly reflected in their reenactment. They continued:

> *"'Tis better far for us to strive*
> *Our useless cares from us to drive;*
> *Do this, and joy your hearts will swell—*
> *All is well! All is well!"*

The second verse began with even more feeling:

> *"Why should we mourn or think our lot is hard?*
> *'Tis not so; all is right.*

Why should we think to earn a great reward
If we now shun the fight?"

There have been few occasions when lyrics have touched me so deeply. With each word I felt the pain and suffering of the early Saints. With each new verse I felt the sorrow of such a journey, the joy and promises of greater rewards, and the blessings that come from such a sacrifice.

"Gird up your loins; fresh courage take.
Our God will never us forsake;
And soon we'll have this tale to tell—
All is well! All is well!"

By the third verse, I could scarcely sing. As I looked around the circled crowd, each person still focused intently on the stone marker, I hardly noticed a dry eye. The song seemed to take us back to a time when early pioneers gathered in similar fashion, mourning the loss of a loved one. Only their pain had been real; ours was in humble remembrance.

"We'll find the place which God for us prepared,
Far away in the West,
Where none shall come to hurt or make afraid;
There the Saints will be blessed."

I couldn't help but sense the extraordinary vision and faith of the early pioneers. They were literally driven and persecuted from city to city, state to state; and through it all they endured the suffering patiently, knowing that eventually they would "find the place which God for us prepared." Once there, as the third verse so eloquently reads, the Saints would

"Make the air with music ring,
Shout praises to our God and King.

Above the rest these words we'll tell—
All is well! All is well!"

The veil was thin on this sacred occasion. The bright morning sun, piercing through the grove of trees, added to the enlightenment we all felt. It was truly a hallowed moment in time, filled with the delicate Spirit of the Lord.

As the fourth verse began, my emotion was too great to allow me to continue. I walked some distance from the crowd and faintly heard the group sing:

"And should we die before our journey's through,
Happy day! All is well!
We then are free from toil and sorrow, too;
With the just we shall dwell!"

Some 6,000 Saints died along this trail. Contemplating this, you couldn't help feeling a small measure of the tremendous losses their families suffered as they buried loved ones and forever left their graves. As this latter-day congregation struggled through the final verse, they too envisioned the afflictions and final rejoicing of the early Saints.

"But if our lives are spared again
To see the Saints their rest obtain,
Oh, how we'll make this chorus swell—
All is well! All is well!" (*Hymns*, No. 30)

When the song ended, there was silence. Only the quiet outpouring of emotion could be heard. Tears streamed down the faces of both men and women; even the children were touched. This was a new congregation that now circled the burial site; their eyes were still focused on the old stone marker, but they were now open to a clearer understanding of what took place along this trail of hope and tears. My eyes had been opened, too. There, on the dusty plains of central Nebraska, hearts were touched, testimonies renewed, and a new spirit of peace born.

I interviewed many of those in attendance, and they shared with me their personal experiences.

"I really felt the presence of my great-great-grandfather," one woman told me.

"This has been the most rewarding experience of the entire journey," another said. "I truly felt the Spirit of the Lord and the presence of my ancestors who traveled these plains."

I understood completely what they were saying. It was an occasion that gave me, too, a new appreciation for our stalwart pioneer ancestors. What great faith they had! What great courage and drive, under the most difficult of circumstances, to find "what God for them prepared." They suffered through countless trials and afflictions, but endured them well. I thank God for their faith.

We can learn much from our pioneer ancestors. Above all, we can learn to overcome, to endure, to be ever constant and faithful. We are pioneers in our own right—modern-day pioneers, forging our way through very different trials and faced with very different challenges. We live in an ever-changing world filled with confusion and sin, where men and women stumble in ignorance and are easily seduced by the "cunning craftiness" of the evil one. Satan, the father of all lies, is working hard to turn men, women, and children away from God. But if we are faithful, we will open new trails that others can follow and look to with glad hearts.

We, too, can be faithful pioneers, leading the way for a latter-day generation of the spiritually blind. The world has great need for shining examples, beacons of light and hope who will be unyielding in their desire to do good and let their lights shine. Let us "look to God and live," finding courage and hope in the same inspired lyrics that have given strength to so many:

> *Why should we mourn or think our lot is hard?*
> *'Tis not so; all is right.*
> *Why should we think to earn a great reward*

If we now shun the fight?
Gird up your loins; fresh courage take.
Our God will never us forsake;
And soon we'll have this tale to tell—
All is well! All is well!

ONE BOY'S FAITH
A Twister's Deadly Pass In Alabama

One early morning in the winter of 1994, I was standing alone in the middle of an old graveyard filled with dozens of tombstones. A light frost layered the visible grave markers, many of them partly covered by overgrown brush and fallen leaves. The burial site was near Piedmont, Alabama, a quiet, rather serene town located in the north-eastern part of the state. I had only a short time before I had to begin my hour-long drive to the airport, but I couldn't leave this small town without first visiting the final resting places of two special members of a family I had come to know over the past couple of days.

As I slowly maneuvered my way around the grave markers, my eyes finally came to rest on the name I was searching for, engraved on a small metal plate pressed into the earth. "Thomas," the name read—not on just one marker, but two. The larger one belonged to Jeffrey, a loving father and devoted husband. The other, positioned over a noticeably smaller burial site, belonged to Sara, Jeffrey's nine-year-old daughter.

My mind began to drift as I gazed down at the two graves. I thought of the tragic events that had brought these good people to their deaths. Here was a young girl, happy and free, and the spunk of the Thomas family. She was the one in the family who seemed to make everyone laugh—her parents' pride and joy, and the darling of the entire neighborhood. She was the little girl down the street whom everyone loved.

To one side of Sara's grave was that of her father. Jeffrey Thomas had been a man in the prime of his life who was known to be a good father to his children, a good husband, and a wonderful provider for his family. He was a God-fearing man and taught his children to love the Lord, to honor and respect others, to pray, read the Bible, and attend church. Ironically, it was during a church service when their lives were taken.

I was in Piedmont to revisit this event, and to tell the world about the Thomas family through the eyes of Ryan Thomas, Sara's fourteen-year-old brother and the couple's only son. Ryan gave me a detailed and emotional account of how he lost his father and sister. You see, he was there; he witnessed the tragedy and, sadly, was involved in it. This is the story of how he survived—not just physically, but spiritually—and how his struggle continues to this day.

According to Ryan, it was a beautiful spring morning in April—Palm Sunday, the week before Easter. The Thomas family was gathered for worship in the Goshen United Methodist Church, along with some sixty other parishioners. It was a time of celebration for them; after all, this was Easter, when messages of a new beginning are often repeated, when remembrances of the Savior's love, atonement, and resurrection are more vivid, and when life itself seems to enjoy a new birth.

The children of the congregation were the focus on this Palm Sunday. They were presenting a special Easter program about the death and resurrection of Jesus Christ. Sara was one of nearly a dozen children participating in the play. Soon after the service started, the program began, music played, and proud parents watched. As the children's performance continued, the weather outside grew progressively worse. It started to rain, and the wind began to blow. Parishioners weren't too alarmed by this sudden change in conditions; although they were aware of how quickly and dangerously weather patterns could change, they were also used to the cyclical changes of Mother Nature's elements in their town.

Not long into the program, the congregation heard a faint thunderous noise that rapidly grew louder and louder. Within seconds, the deafening roar was so loud and violent that it seemed to shake the very foundation of the little chapel. This was no ordinary rain and wind storm, Ryan thought. This was something awful.

As he told me the story, Ryan admitted the noise scared him. He wanted to slide out of the church pew and look out the window, but by then it was too late. Before he was able to move, a category-4 tornado with 200-mile-per-hour winds made a direct hit on the chapel. The small brick church was no match for the monstrous twister; the tornado cut a swath right through the middle of the chapel, scattering everything and everyone over a two-block area. Within seconds the small church came crashing down, crumbling under the force of the storm.

After the tornado passed there was only an eerie, frightening silence. But it didn't last long; soon children's cries could be heard, then the screams of mothers searching for their children and fathers calling for their families. Buried beneath bricks, wood, glass, and broken church pews were nearly three dozen members of the congregation, including Ryan, Sara, and their parents.

Ryan was the first in his family to shove aside the debris and slowly get up. He was bruised, cut, and bloody, but able to hear the cries of his sister, who was only a few feet from him. Lifting the bricks from her badly torn body, he was shocked at what he saw: large, open wounds everywhere on her head, chest, and legs. "There was blood all over the place," he said. "I was crying and praying she would live."

When Ryan finished removing the debris from his sister, he knelt beside her and cradled her head in his arms. The falling

bricks had crushed nearly every part of her little body. Ryan could hardly recognize his own sister. He stared at her for what seemed like an eternity, watching, waiting, and hoping for any signs of life. "I was waiting for her to move or to breathe," he said. With tears streaming down his face he cried for help, praying even louder that his sister would live. "Sara! Sara!" he screamed. Nobody heard him, or at least he felt as if no one was listening. There was such chaos surrounding him that Ryan's calls for help just seem to blend into the mass of hysteria. "She was dying in my arms," he said. "I couldn't do anything but watch her die."

Soon, nine-year-old Sara's life slowly slipped away. She was dead. Ryan sat for a moment and cried, then gently laid his sister's head back against the concrete debris and began a slow crawl over and under the twisted rubble, searching for his father. He found Jeffrey buried deep beneath a pile of debris. "I reached for my father to see if he was alive, and that's the last thing I remember."

Ryan collapsed and fainted from a combination of shock, loss of blood, deep lacerations, and a host of other reasons. The next thing he remembered was three days later, when he found himself lying on his back in a hospital bed. A white sheet covered his frail body from the neck down, and a few men were standing around him.

"Where's my mom?" he asked. Other questions quickly followed. "What about my dad and my sister?" Ryan was then told the tragic story of his family. His father and sister were dead, and his mother was hospitalized in critical condition.

Ryan didn't attend his father and sister's funeral. He was hospitalized for nearly two weeks, and did not have the strength to leave his room. He didn't even realize how serious his mother's injuries were until he was released from the hospital and learned that she was in the intensive care unit suffering from punctured organs and other deep lacerations. She was being kept alive by machines, and doctors warned Ryan that she might not live.

If anyone had reason to feel alone, Ryan did. He had lost his father and sister, and for a time thought he was going to lose his mother. Adding to his pain and loneliness was the fact that many of his close friends had died in the tornado, and others were still hospitalized. Eighteen members of the congregation—six children and fourteen adults—had lost their lives.

I spent nearly the entire day speaking with Ryan about this difficult experience. We sat and talked in his living room, where his family had gathered to read the Bible; we walked outside near the old wooden fence, where he and his dad had played ball; and we sat in his sister's bedroom, where he said he loved to tease her repeatedly. His was a story of tremendous struggle, confusion, and often anger. Here was a young fourteen-year-old boy, faced with one of life's most difficult trials: the unexplainable loss of loved ones resulting from a seemingly unexplainable tragedy. At the end of the day, as I was preparing to leave my new friend, I turned and asked him one final question. "Ryan," I said, "what has helped you through this? What, more than anything else, has given you hope and kept your spirits up? If you could sum it up in a few words, what would they be?"

He paused. His eyes grew wet with tears, which began to slowly course down his cheeks. Ryan looked into my eyes for a moment, then bowed his head and cried. After giving my question some thought, he slowly lifted his head, still teary-eyed, and calmly said, "Faith. Faith in God. That's what has helped me through."

I was not expecting this answer. I was expecting him to talk about his relatives, who had given such a generous amount of love and support, or perhaps his own inner strength that had helped him through these heart-wrenching trials. But instead, what came from the mouth of this boy was a true, heartfelt answer. In the midst of death and despair, it was faith in God that had helped Ryan live.

Oh, that each of us could have such faith! Ryan knew something of death; unfortunately, he was surrounded by it. But he also knew something of life; he knew that God had granted it. What I witnessed in this young man was not only a deep, loving respect for God, but a sure knowledge that God would also provide him with comfort and peace.

It was the morning after my visit with Ryan that I found myself alone at his family's burial site. As I looked upon the grave markers of the Thomas family, I thanked the Lord for a boy's faith—a faith powerful enough to provide Ryan the anchor he needed, yet simple enough to teach me about the strength of youth. Considering the great loss this boy had suffered, I was amazed at his stature, at his fortitude, and at his strength to move forward.

I looked at my watch. Time had passed quickly, and I had a plane to catch to Miami. It was December; snow flurries were beginning to fall, and Christmas would be arriving soon. I thought about myself returning home for the holidays to a loving wife and five healthy, beautiful children; and here, in this remote town, a young boy would be left alone. His father and sister were dead, his mother still in serious condition and hardly mobile.

A deep trial of faith had begun for this young man, and no doubt there would be many struggles ahead for Ryan; I prayed silently that he would be able to endure them. But I was comforted by the fact that he had already demonstrated his deep faith in God, and I had every reason to believe he would endure his coming difficulties well. I was most encouraged by what he told me just before I left his home.

As he was sitting in his living room, near a dimly lit Christmas tree, he pointed to a couple of red and white stockings laid at the foot of the small spruce. Each had a name printed neatly at its top. One read, *Sara*. The other read, *Dad*.

"I'll be all right," Ryan told me in a near whisper. "I still have my family. They're just not with me right now."

PART THREE

"WHAT 'ERE THOU ART, ACT WELL THY PART"

If everyone truly understood who they were and from whence they came, this world would be a far better place to live.

"WHAT 'ERE THOU ART, ACT WELL THY PART"

FOREWORD

One of the most profound experiences of my life was my mission. I can clearly remember the day—April 22, 1982—when a friend dropped me off at the Missionary Training Center. There I stood, alone, staring at the building, realizing that the moment I walked through the front doors I would be in the custody of The Church of Jesus Christ of Latter-day Saints. I would be in the Lord's hands, his full-time servant and a preacher of his restored truths. It was an exciting time for me, but it was also a time of nervousness, apprehension, and uncertainty about the challenges that lay ahead.

I picked up my suitcases and made my way toward the front door. As I entered the foyer of the MTC, I saw a rather large stone placed in the center of the room, a monument that had an inscription upon it. It read: "What 'ere thou art, act well thy part." At first glance I didn't think much of the aphorism, but as I walked away, I turned back and read it again, this time taking note of each word.

"What 'ere thou art, act well thy part." Chills ran up and down my spine. Goose bumps covered my arms. I felt the Lord's spirit rest upon me. I'll never forget it; the moment was powerful, and I felt like the Lord was trying to enlighten me. I read it again and again. *What am I?* I thought. *A missionary? A servant of the Lord? A son of righteous parents? A child of a loving God? A young man hungry for the Spirit's teachings?*

Yes, I told myself, *I am all of these.*

Then, if so, how must I act? was my next question. The answer was clear enough, and can easily be found in the scriptures.

When the Lord was asked a similar question, he answered it with a question and answer of his own: "What manner of men ought ye to be? Even as I am" (3 Nephi 27:27).

Yes, I silently told myself. *This is what I must do! This must be my goal!*

I have often thought of this experience, and I realize now more than ever the powerful influence those words had on me. I was young and inexperienced, yet extremely impressionable and yearning for truth and clarity of gospel principles. I was ready, willing, and anxious to preach the restored gospel of our Lord; but I needed, as all young missionaries do, experiences that enlighten one's understanding about who we really are.

The inscription reminded President David O. McKay of who he was many years ago when he was serving a mission in Sterling, Scotland. He was so uplifted by the adage that he wrote down the inscription, which now sits in replica in the Missionary Training Center. One day, when Elder McKay was feeling gloomy and homesick, he happened to come across this proverb engraved in stone upon the entryway to a large home. He read it again and again and realized the power in the words. The experience was so influential that it changed the course of Elder McKay's mission. It reminded him of who he was and gave him the motivation necessary to eagerly do the Lord's work. Similarly, the statement seemed to give me the boost and inspiration I needed during the early days of my mission.

The inscription also reminded me of something my sweet mother often told me. "Remember who you are," she would say as I went running off to school or to a friend's house. Her gentle reminders were constant throughout my life, even when I left home for Ricks College, my mission, and later Brigham Young University.

"Remember who you are." However trite I initially thought this adage was, I later learned of its deeper meaning and often found myself reflecting upon it. The engraving on the stone monument only seemed to reinforce my mother's words and help build the cornerstone of my mission. To this day, both my mother's gentle reminder and the inscription in the foyer of the

MTC have reminded me of the importance of recognizing who we really are.

If the inhabitants of the world truly understood that they are literally sons and daughters of a loving God, created in his image, and that they have the potential to become like him, can you imagine how different today's world would be? Such knowledge would grant hope to countless individuals who are now living in uncertainty, confusion, and despair.

Once we understand our divine origins, we must make every effort to return to our loving Father in Heaven, to obey his commandments, and to share his love with others. The plan of salvation offers each of us the agency and opportunity to do so. Great blessings await the children of God who recognize who they truly are and "act well thy part."

"Because It's True!"
A Boy's Example on the Wagon Train

When I travel to various locations, especially out of the country, our crew often hires what is called a "fixer." This is a person who doubles as a driver, is knowledgeable about the surroundings and familiar with the fastest way of arriving at any given location, has established contacts, and is generally someone the crew depends upon a great deal.

The primary responsibility of the fixer is to simply "fix" or arrange whatever the correspondent and crew need to put the story together. Fixers are almost always used when rushing into foreign countries, but they are rarely used domestically. There was one occasion, however, when the need for a domestic fixer came in quite handy.

I was asked to do a story on the modern-day Mormon wagon train as it made its way across the plains. Several hundred Latter-day Saints, history buffs, and wagoners were celebrating the sesquicentennial of the pioneers' arrival in the Salt Lake Valley by reenacting the great migration of 1847. The entourage of wagons and handcarts was on its fourth week of a three-month journey to Utah.

My producer and I flew out of Miami to meet the train just west of North Platte, Nebraska. The camera crew arrived from an entirely different location. After catching up with the group of wagons, we determined it would be impossible to follow the wagon train, carry equipment, and keep in touch with wagon leaders, unless we had a good fixer who could double as our driver.

We found such a person. He was the son of the chairman of the wagon train. He knew the central plains of Nebraska, knew the most colorful people to talk to, was familiar with the route of the train, and was a member of the LDS Church. He was the perfect fixer. There was only one minor concern. We had some rough terrain to travel. This boy was only sixteen years old, and had been driving for only a couple of months. We hired him anyway.

Our fixer's name was Les. He was a nice young man, extremely helpful, always cheerful and willing to take care of whatever minor problems cropped up. He lacked skills in only one area: driving. Actually, he wasn't a bad driver; we survived the bumpy ride, even if the terrain caused us some headaches. There were some fairly steep grades of sand hills and prairie ruts that we had to maneuver through. At least Les had a good time driving.

Les knew very little about the CBS crew he was hired to drive for. For starters, I'm confident he never thought any of us were members of the LDS Church. In fact, my producer and camera crew made it a point to clear up any speculation that they might be members. I never mentioned that I was LDS, and I'm sure my interrogation of him probably cleared up any thoughts he had of my being a Mormon.

After the standard, formal introductions, I charged in with my first question, asked with almost a tone of disgust in my voice. "So, Les," I said, "Are you one of these Mormons?"

He laughed, then responded matter-of-factly. "Yes, I am. Why?"

My questions continued. "Well, do you like being one of these Mormons?" I said, as if I despised them.

"Yeah, I do," he said. "It's great. My whole family belongs to the Mormon Church."

"Oh," I said while glancing through the paper and appearing less than interested in the conversation. "It sounds like a boring thing to do."

"Not at all," he replied. Then he went into a rambling description of all the fun Mormons have.

So far, my questions did not seem to disconcert the young man. He handled all of them with ease. Here was a young man talking to complete strangers from CBS News and not showing a bit of shyness about his beliefs. After giving him a short rest, I made an attempt to frazzle him as my questioning became more belligerent. "Aren't there too many rules for Mormons to follow? Aren't there just too many commandments you have to live by?" I asked. I was expecting him to cave in just a little, or at least be somewhat intimidated by the question and agree with me in part. I was fooled.

"There are a lot of commandments," he said. "It's not easy being a Mormon, but all the rules are for your own good. By following the commandments, you'll be a happier and healthier person."

"Hmm," I grumbled. "Can't a person be happy and not live these commandments? Are you saying Mormons are the only truly happy people?"

"No," he said, "but not everyone who thinks he is happy is really happy. Also, if you want to be eternally happy, you have to be a Mormon."

"Right, right," I said. He was so bold! I gave him a surprised look in response to his courageous answer, but deep inside I was saying to myself, *Yes! Yes! Yes! What a stalwart!* Here was a youth living up to his noble birthright! What a terrific standard-bearer of truth! He was holding his head high, not succumbing to the whims of society or crumbling under the pressure of a correspondent's questions. I was pleased. I was very, very pleased.

I looked at him for a moment, somewhat ashamed for not letting him know I was a member of the Church; but I just had to question him a while longer. I wasn't trying to embarrass or bully him; I was simply curious about where today's average Mormon youth stood. I couldn't blow my cover just yet.

The day passed quickly. I was in and out of the vehicle several times, my photographer and producer were hopping from wagon to wagon, and our trusty driver Les was handling his duties quite well. Occasionally, when I was in the vehicle, I would pop him a question or two about the wagon train or some of its participants. He handled every question with extreme ease and confidence.

At one point, after asking several questions about the wagon train and why anyone would want to participate in such a difficult journey, I commented out loud for Les's benefit, "Boy, what a bunch of crazy Mormons!"

"Crazy?" he responded. "Many of these people aren't even members of the Mormon Church, and those who are, are doing this because our history is important. They want to understand and go through what our ancestors did."

My new friend had an answer for everything. I loved it. Les never became confrontational or argumentative. He was always courteous, thoughtful, and quick to speak up in defense of the Church. He was a true missionary.

By the end of the day, I felt like I knew Les quite well. To me, he was a brave, bold young man, proud of his membership in the Lord's kingdom and certainly willing to share his testimony of it with strangers. Because of my tone of questioning, he probably didn't think of me as any friend of the Church. So far, I had him fooled; but I thought it was time he should know the truth.

The day was nearly over. Les, my producer and I were in the vehicle. Les was in the driver's seat, and I was on the passenger's side. The questioning began in earnest. "So what other things do you have to do when you're a Mormon?" I asked. I was wondering what sort of answer he would give, knowing that it would only be bait for further questioning.

"Well," he said, "we go to seminary in the morning."

"Seminary? What's that?" I asked.

"It's like a bible school every morning. It starts at six o'clock. We study the scriptures, learn about the Church, sing songs, and pray."

I was surprised at his openness and impressed with his boldness. I quietly cheered him on, hoping and silently praying that he wouldn't break under this interrogation. Meanwhile, my producer sat quietly in the backseat, thumbing through a two-day-old newspaper and probably wondering why I would be asking this boy so many questions about the Church.

Just one more line of questioning, I thought. *Just a few more questions.*

"So, Les," I said, "Are you going on one of those Mormon missions?"

He laughed. "One of those Mormon missions, huh?" he said. "Why, of course!"

"Of course?" I questioned. "Why would you want to do that? Wouldn't you rather be doing other things a normal nineteen-year-old would be doing?"

He paused. It was obvious he was thinking this answer through. After his brief hesitation he said with a calm but firm voice, "I want to go on a mission because I know it's true. I know the teachings of the Mormon Church are true and will make others happy."

Yes! I silently told myself. That was enough. I had learned all I needed to know about one young man's faith. His answers to all my questions could be summed up in those five beautiful, simple words, "because I know it's true."

After his answer, my producer, in a rather loud, rebuking tone, spoke up. "Art, why do you keep pestering this boy with your questions?" She then looked at Les. "Les, don't you know that Art is a member of the Mormon Church?"

Les froze. He turned bright red. His mouth opened, but no words came. His eyes grew big as he stared at me and tried to mumble a few barely comprehensible words. "You mean you're a member of the Church?"

"Yes," I admitted. "Les, I apologize for deceiving you."

I began to feel terrible for misleading my new friend. I had placed him in an unfair position. But, I must say, by doing so I had learned a great deal about the strength of this young man's testimony.

"Les," I repeated, "Again, I am sorry for not telling you the whole truth, but I want you to know how proud I am of you." I went on. "You represented the Church in a most admirable way, and you are to be commended. The Lord's kingdom is in good hands when he has young men like you as his next generation of leaders."

I was speaking the truth. I wasn't attempting to flatter Les; my heart had been touched by his sincere faithfulness, his willingness to bear testimony, and his burning desire to speak in courageous defense of the Lord's kingdom. I hope every young man and woman would do the same under similar questioning, and that every member of the Church would follow the example of this fine young man.

We should all ask ourselves occasionally, "What would I say? What would I do?" If at some point in our lives we are confronted with such intense interrogation about our personal lives and beliefs, I would hope that we could be as forthright as Les in standing for truth and right.

THE MOST IMPORTANT QUESTION
A Visit to Ricks College

I graduated from Ricks College in December of 1981. Since then, I have been invited to return on a couple of occasions to speak at the college's Education Forums. It's always a pleasure to return to the school where I like to think it all began. It was and still is a wonderful institution, and both my wife and I have fond memories of our time there. Our visits have only rekindled the love we share for the school.

Not long ago, I returned to Ricks College for a speaking engagement and met a professor I hadn't seen in many, many years. His name is Kay Wilkins; he's been retired now for a number of years, but was a long-time communications and journalism instructor at Ricks. When I began my schooling at the college in the fall of 1980, he was the first professor I met and the one I grew closest to through my association with the Journalism Department.

After a morning meeting with administrators, I talked with a couple of classes about my experiences in covering Latin America and the Caribbean. By noon, I had been deluged with questions from students, professors, and administrators about every aspect of journalism. It seems you never stop answering inquiries about life, work, family, and ambitions during these visits, but I've always considered it an honor to participate, and I thoroughly enjoy the experience.

It was just before my official lunch with the president of Ricks College that I met Mr. Wilkins. He had been invited to the noon gathering along with several other current and former professors. I was surrounded by these individuals when Kay Wilkins approached. I immediately recognized him. "Brother Wilkins!" I said, pleasantly surprised that he was in attendance. "It's so good to see you."

He looked terrific, hardly a day older than when we had last met. He smiled broadly, extending one hand for a firm shake and placing the other on my shoulder. Then, looking me sternly in the eyes, he said, "I know it's been years since I've seen you, Art, but my first and most important question is this: What are you doing in the Lord's church today?"

Of all the questions to be asked, my current standing in the Lord's kingdom was most important to this good man. He knew my response would be a telling signal of my faithfulness. If I was true, then he wanted to know it; and if I wasn't, he wanted to know that, too—and I'm confident he would have been the first to call me to repentance.

I must admit to being startled by his question. I'd been asked literally dozens of questions that morning, none dealing with my Church standing, so his inquiry caught me off guard. But, with our hands still locked, I looked at him and smiled, feeling good that my answer would not be disappointing. "I am happily serving as a stake high councilor," I told him, "and my lovely wife is serving in the Young Women's organization. We have five beautiful, happy, and healthy children. The Lord has blessed us greatly."

"That is good," he said with a soft, approving voice. We went on to talk about experiences of the past several years, about life in southern Florida, and about work at CBS News.

Later that night, I visited with Brother Wilkins and his beautiful wife in their comfortable, modest home just two blocks west of Ricks College. The couple showed me some lovely portraits of the family; they had four daughters and one son. They proudly walked me through the house, showing me framed pictures of their extended family, which, of course, included a host of photographs of their numerous grandchildren.

We talked about family, about retired life, about my former professor's decades of work at Ricks College. Brother Wilkins admittedly missed the association he had once enjoyed with his students, and the pleasure of being so involved in the study of journalism. But the driving force now, as he explained, was watching his posterity bloom and grow. He was spending greater and more quality time with loved ones, and was giving of his time, talents, and energy to the service of others. He was surrounding himself with and truly relishing all that is of the greatest worth in our busy lives: the Church and our individual families.

As I left my professor's house that evening and rested comfortably in my hotel room, I thought of the day's events. It was not the speech, the discussions in class, or the accolades I received from others that would be most remembered. It was, instead, the meek and soft-spoken way of a professor who demonstrated, by example, the more important things in life.

So often in our time-pressured lives, as we attempt to make a living, racing from business meeting to board meeting, conference to convention, client to associate, state to state, and country to country, we get so wrapped up in life's perishables that we fail to pause and reflect on that which is truly enduring. Even at home, our time is consumed by never-ending household chores. We wash and scrub, wipe and mop, dust and pick up, wash this and that, only to do it again tomorrow. We fill our afternoons with children's homework and science projects, and we hustle our little ones and adolescents to and from sports practices and games, gymnastics meets, school gatherings and, of course, the never-ending birthday parties. We begin to feel like taxi drivers without the monetary tips. Life, it seems, takes on an interesting beat of its own in the endless cycle of doing this and that. Soon we feel more like machines than thoughtful individuals. If we don't exercise some degree of caution in this frenzied, chaotic atmosphere, any attributes of brotherly kindness and temperance seem to disappear. Household tension escalates, patience is lost, and contention erupts far too easily. Eventually, the things we should truly cherish become secondary to the daily grinds of life.

What we are desperately searching for, but too often never find, is a daily moment of peace—a moment in which we can call upon a higher power to lighten our loads and ease our burdens. A moment of true reflection, during which we invite the Lord's spirit into our hearts and homes, granting us direction and reminding us of our priorities. If we fail to find or make the time for such moments, we unintentionally allow a spirit of discord into the home and an accusatory spirit into our hearts. The once constant promptings of the Holy Ghost slowly fade until the family is left with the uninspired teachings of a husband and wife. Nothing can be more damaging. On the other hand, lasting solace and true happiness and peace come only through living the gospel of Jesus Christ.

The good professor reminded me of this during our visit. It was something I clearly understood; even so, one cannot be taught enough about such things. The scriptures are replete with examples of those who slowly begin losing the vision of their true goal. They slip from the iron rod and are lost in the fog of despair. One of the clearest and most direct scriptural reminders about this very subject can be found in the New Testament. When the Lord was delivering the Sermon on the Mount, he spoke a few simple but eternally profound words: "Seek ye first the kingdom of God, and his righteousness, and all things shall be added unto you" (Matthew 6:33).

There is no clearer directive or more lucid command. These eighteen words offer the perfect summary of what our mortal objective should be. They are words that speak truth—words that my good professor obviously had in mind when he asked, "What are you doing in the Lord's church today?"

HOT, DRY, AND THIRSTY IN HAITI
A Brush with Caffeine

It was a hot fall day in the mid-1990s, and the drive from the western coastal town of Gonaives, Haiti, to Port-au-Prince seemed to take hours. The distance was only about seventy miles, but the road conditions and traffic in Haiti made it feel like seven hundred. It was awful. I was in the front seat of an old, rickety truck, feeling every monstrous bump and pothole in the road. In Haiti, you can't drive ten feet without running over one—and that's when driving conditions are at their best. Most of the time, we traveled on dirt roads so dry and parched that even the smallest vehicle created a dust storm too thick to see through. To make matters worse, our vehicle didn't have air conditioning; so, in a crude attempt at bringing in fresh air, we kept our windows rolled down. At least it helped circulate the dust and exhaust we were breathing.

We had spent the day running from township to village, talking to Haitians about the upcoming presidential elections. This was a milestone in Haitian history—the first free democratic elections in many, many years. My assignment was to report on the struggle to build democracy in this country that had witnessed precious little of it. Most people here handled their problems with violence and bloodshed, tactics which had long been promoted by ruthless and brutal dictators. To put the country's problems in the simplest of terms; its economy lacked any form of infrastructure to promote development and growth, let alone build roads to allow vehicles to travel. Such conveniences as the corner food market or fast-food restaurants simply didn't exist. There was no running water, very little electricity, and rations of food for the average Haitian were less than adequate. Haitians died on the street every day from dehydration. Knowing this, whenever we left our hotel in Port-au-Prince to travel the country, we would try to pack enough food and liquid for the trip. I can only remember one occasion when our resources ran out, or at least mine did. It was during this trip from Gonaives to Port-au-Prince.

In the trunk of our sport utility vehicle were two large coolers loaded with ice, sandwiches, and plenty of drinks. The drinks usually consisted of various brands of soda, several cans of beer, and for me, fruit juice and a whole case of bottled water. My colleagues are all aware of my drinking habits and are quite familiar with my standards as a member of the Church. Some called me the token conservative at CBS, and one who has reminded my colleagues many times of my standards and morals. Fortunately, they have always been considerate enough to warn me before any bad jokes are spoken, apologize after swearing, and generally respect my beliefs—helping me, in fact, to live as I should. They always seem to go out of their way to purchase juice and water.

The road to Port-au-Prince was not only hot and dry, but long and rough. It was a tedious drive in what was already an exhausting day of gathering pictures and interviewing various individuals. My throat was so dry I could hardly swallow. Dust filled my nostrils, and I reeked of sweat. Everyone in the vehicle did. When in Haiti, you always expected to finish the day hot, sweaty, and covered with a layer of filth. Water and juice kept me moving, but unfortunately my supply was running low.

"Could you hand me another bottle of water?" I asked my photographer, who was seated in the backseat.

"It's your last one," he said, then joked, "Looks like you'll have to break down and have a beer soon."

I took the water and drank it slowly, knowing it would be several hours before I would be able to purchase more.

We soon arrived at our makeshift office in Port-au-Prince, and began scrambling to put our story together. As the correspondent, my job was to watch the interviews, script out the best sound bites from the interviews, be familiar with my video, and write the story. On this occasion, however, my parched throat was so dry and my body so dehydrated that I found it hard to concentrate.

"Is there any more water or juice in either of those coolers?" I asked my producer, knowing what the answer would be.

"Nothing here but a few bottles of beer and a can of Pepsi," he said. Then he added with a smirk, "Come on, Art, put a little alcohol or caffeine into your system. It will help you write." He laughed.

There wasn't even any ice left in the cooler; by now it had melted into a cloudy, milky liquid with plenty of "floaties" in it.

Time was growing short. I had less than an hour to write the script and send it to New York for approval before we could start the video editing process. While I was writing, my producer and editor both walked out of the room. I looked over at the cooler and told myself, *Here's my chance! I'll grab the can of Pepsi, drink it before they return, and they'll never know.*

I walked to the cooler and opened the lid. When you're hot, dry, and longing for something to quench your thirst, even foul-looking water is appealing. I was tempted to cup my hands and drink it, but instead settled for something that had a much more desirable taste: the only can of Pepsi. I pulled the can out of the water and walked back to my small writing table. But halfway there, I turned back; it just didn't feel right. The Spirit's promptings were reminding me of the many times I had refused caffeine drinks from my colleagues based upon my religious convictions. It was clear in my mind that if my colleagues found out, the consequences would not be pretty. I followed the direction of the Spirit and placed the Pepsi back in the cooler, then returned to my writing.

Twenty or thirty minutes passed, and I was nearly finished with my script. It was quiet, with no sign of my producer, editor, photographer, or soundman anywhere. *This is my chance,* I told myself again. Ignoring what I knew would be the right thing to do, I walked to the cooler, quickly grabbed the can of Pepsi, and popped the lid. It made a cool, refreshing sound. I hurried back to my writing table and placed the can in an inconspicuous spot—under a towel next to my laptop computer. *No one would ever notice it here,* I thought. I was making every effort to not get caught.

Before long, my producer and photography crew returned. "How's the script coming? We need to start editing this piece," my producer said.

"Done," I told him. The producer glanced over the script, said it looked good, and we sent it by computer modem to New York. Fifteen minutes later I was on the phone with an executive producer in New York, going over a few minor changes in the story. After final approval, I printed the "to-air" version and we began the video editing. During this process, I kept a close watch on the white towel next to my computer—the one covering the Pepsi can. When I was confident no one was watching, I would casually walk back to my corner writing table, remove the towel, and take a drink.

It was six o'clock, half an hour before the national *CBS Evening News* was scheduled to air. We were frantically making last-minute changes to cut eight seconds out of our story. It gets pretty wild when we're pressed for time, which always seems to be the case. I was pacing the floor of our crude little office while the editor was shuttling through video in a near frenzy, pressing buttons and swearing at the editing machines because of a few minor quirks that always seemed to delay us. Occasionally, in my anxiety, I would sneak over to my corner and take a sip of my soda. Meantime, my producer, who had traveled throughout the world with CBS News for twelve years, stood quietly behind the editor, chewing his gum and even blowing a few bubbles. "We'll make it," he said. "I'll call New York and tell them we'll feed the piece at 6:25."

"Feeding the piece" is a phrase which means the edited version of the story is sent by satellite to the New York transmission room. The piece is then transferred to another room and placed in a machine, where a technician stands ready to press the "play" button when Dan Rather says, "Art Rascon has more from Haiti."

"We don't have much time left!" I said. "How are we doing?" It was a rhetorical question, but one that I always asked anxiously as we approached our feed time.

"Just one last picture to edit," yelled the editor. "We'll make it. We'll make it." I've heard those words many, many times throughout my career. Even though they have proven true ninety-eight percent of the time, I still get quite nervous and wear down a small, ten-foot section of the floor with my pacing.

The editor slapped his hands on his working desk. "Finished!" he proclaimed, pulling the tape from the machine and holding it in the air.

I seized the opportunity for one last gulp of Pepsi, grabbed the tape, and ran out the door with my producer right behind me. We raced to a waiting vehicle, jumped in, and sped off to the transmission location about two miles away. The satellite dish was placed on the roof of the finest hotel in Haiti, but the building had no elevator—not a surprise in this country. We jumped out of the vehicle, ran into the hotel, and began leaping stairs, skipping two or three with each jump. At the top was a large tent housing the uplink dish and transmission equipment. "CBS is here," my producer shouted.

"You have four minutes," the satellite technician said matter-of-factly, emphasizing each word while lifting four fingers of his hand. He wanted to make sure we understood. On a story such as this, where other networks are also slotted for satellite time, it's imperative that you feed during your scheduled satellite "window." If you miss your window, you are literally at the mercy of another network, and may find yourself on your knees, begging for a few minutes of their satellite time to feed your story. I'm not exaggerating; I've seen it happen many times. Missing your feed time for a major story is a very serious offense, and New York executives usually don't take it lightly.

Fortunately, we arrived with a few minutes left in our window. The editor placed the tape in the deck, pressed "play," and we watched the monitor as the two-minute story was sent to New York. The editor was on the phone with technicians, who were capturing the piece and making certain the audio and video levels looked good. "We have the piece!" New York said.

"Got to go, we have to turn it around." New York quickly hung up the phone.

The story aired on the national *CBS News with Dan Rather* program only minutes after we fed it. What a relief! It made its time slot, and everyone seemed pleased with the story. I can't count how many times I've been through this process in various places throughout the world, and yet my nerves are always on edge until the piece is successfully fed. Once it airs, a tremendous burden is lifted from my shoulders. The pressure is off, and I slowly begin to unwind from what usually is a fourteen-hour day.

Once back in our office, I got rid of the "evidence." I dumped the empty Pepsi can into a large bag of garbage and sealed it. Later that evening, my colleagues and I went to dinner at one of three locations where we believed it was safe to eat. Right in the middle of an otherwise pleasant conversation, my producer interrupted with a rather startling comment. "Hey, Art," he said, "you know what? Your prophet wouldn't be very happy with you today."

I was shocked. What had I done or said that would cause my producer to say something like that?

He went on. "You didn't think I noticed you drinking that can of Pepsi, did you? I saw you trying to hide the can. You didn't fool me."

I was embarrassed and humiliated. Everything I had ever said, every time I had tried to be an example of the gospel, seemed to be an accusation against me. The rest of my colleagues at the dinner table actually looked stunned.

"You mean you finally drank that can of Pepsi?" one asked, laughing. "We were wondering whether you ever would." They laughed some more. It became a real joke.

"So, it's okay to have caffeine drinks if you're real thirsty? Is that it? What about beer, Art? Is that the next drink?" another taunted.

They all had a good laugh, but I didn't find it funny. In those few moments, I recognized the damage that had been done—not only to my reputation, but to members of the Church everywhere. I turned to my colleagues at the table and quieted their levity with these simple words: "I'm sorry."

I was genuinely apologetic. I felt horrible. I knew I had gone against the Spirit's direction, and against all that I had previously told them about the Word of Wisdom. I was now suffering the consequences of my weakness. It was as if the pedestal they had placed me on had suddenly collapsed, and I fell flat on my face. I apologized again. "I'm sorry," I said. "I shouldn't have been drinking the Pepsi, and I promise you I won't do it again."

Unfortunately, forgiveness hasn't come easy among my colleagues. To this day, they still laugh and joke about it.

This experience made me realize the tremendous importance of upholding the values that we all profess to believe in. There is no question that members of the Church are watched more closely than any other group of people. Do you think for a moment that a member of another religious affiliation would be rebuked for drinking a can of Pepsi? I think not.

As a correspondent for the news media, I'm acutely aware of this phenomenon. In my reading of papers and news magazines, I occasionally come across a story where an individual's religious affiliation is mentioned, and it generally seems to occur when the individual in question is a member of the LDS Church. In the print and broadcast media, these words echo almost louder than the alleged indiscretion: "So and so, *who is a member of the Mormon Church…*"

Do you ever wonder why such distinctions are made? It's clear in my mind, and in many ways I view the distinction as more of a compliment than an indictment. By and large, the media consider Mormons a group of people who pride themselves on living clean, healthy lifestyles, complete with standards of moral integrity, honesty, and deeply rooted family values. The LDS affiliation is usually mentioned only because the professed standards of the person in question are obviously contradicted by his actions. In other words, in the reporter's eyes, the individual should have been living the high standards of the Mormon Church, but instead is facing a serious accusation.

I believe most media people respect Mormons' disciplined living—so much, in fact, that when a member of the Church fails to live up to these standards, it's definitely worth mentioning. There are those, of course, whose only motive is to discredit or destroy the reputation of the Church. Some even write lengthy articles on trivial matters in which a Mormon has been involved, while others write entire books in an attempt to lead away true believers or prospective members of the Church. These "journalists," if they can call themselves that, will never win. Their efforts to thwart the work of the Lord are in vain. The Prophet Joseph Smith once proclaimed:

> No unhallowed hand can stop the work from progressing; persecutions may rage, mobs may combine, armies may assemble, calumny may defame, but the truth of God will go forth boldly, nobly, and independent, till it has penetrated every continent, visited every clime, swept every country, and sounded in every ear, till the purposes of God shall be accomplished, and the Great Jehovah shall say the work is done. (*History of The Church of Jesus Christ of Latter-day Saints* [Salt Lake City: Deseret Book Company, 1978], vol. 4, p. 540.)

What a wonderful promise and reassurance from the Lord regarding any efforts to thwart his important latter-day work.

I like to look upon the frequent attention the Mormons receive in today's media as a clear reflection of how influential the Church and its members have become throughout the world. Society recognizes that Latter-day Saints live much higher standards than most of the general population. Do we dare disappoint them? Or, more importantly, do we dare disappoint the Lord? I would hope not; and yet, we all have our frailties, faults, and weaknesses. The critical element is our desire and effort to change and grow in positive ways.

Although my brief flirtation with a can of Pepsi in Haiti occurred some time ago, and was only a minor indiscretion, its impact has not been forgotten. To this day, when some small event has not gone my way, such as a story that's been canceled, a flat tire, or whatever it might be, there is an inevitable comment from someone in the office: "It's that Pepsi in Haiti, Art. The Lord's still punishing you. You should never have caved in."

I freely admit that the Pepsi incident was a break in my character; but it certainly made a lasting impression, and helped me realize the powerful influence members of the Church can have on the lives of others. "True to the Faith"... it's a motto we all need to live by.

"Serve a Mission"
Learning at the Feet of an Apostle

Some time ago, while vacationing in Utah, Patti and I and our children had the wonderful opportunity of meeting with Elder M. Russell Ballard, an Apostle of The Church of Jesus Christ of Latter-day Saints. Elder Ballard had officiated at our marriage and sealing ceremony back on August 21, 1985. He was serving as a member of the First Quorum of Seventy at the time, and was called as an Apostle later that year.

My family was touring the sights at Temple Square when Patti and I decided to check Elder Ballard's office to see if he was in. Our visit was not scheduled, but he was kind enough to visit with us for a few moments. The family stood quietly in the lobby as I asked the front security guard to ring his office. He did so, and was told by a secretary to have the family take the elevator to a designated floor.

We waited briefly in Elder Ballard's reception area before he emerged from his office. We respectfully stood, and my wife and I exchanged greetings with him. Elder Ballard was extremely gracious to allow our family this visit, and we thanked him for the opportunity. We then turned to our children and began to introduce them.

"Our eldest son is Jacob," I said. Before I could say more, Elder Ballard turned to Jacob and extended his hand for a shake. Looking him directly in the eyes, Elder Ballard asked his first question of the family.

"How old are you, Jacob?"

"I'm ten years old," he responded with a nervous smile on his face. I think he knew what the next question was going to be.

"Are you preparing for a mission?" Elder Ballard asked firmly but lovingly.

"Yes!" Jacob said.

I breathed a sigh of relief. My son had responded pleasantly and correctly.

After introducing the other four children, we stepped into his office, comfortably sat down, and began discussing other matters. A few minutes later, a knock came at Elder Ballard's door. "Come in," he said. It was Robert L. Backman, a former member of the Quorum of the Seventy and a prominent leader in the Boy Scouts of America. "Meet the Rascon family," Elder Ballard said as he began introducing us.

After the formal introductions, Elder Backman turned first to Jacob and looked him sternly in the eyes. "Jacob, how old are you?" he asked.

"I'm ten," Jacob responded.

"What are you going to be doing nine years from now, Jacob?" Elder Backman asked in his familiar bold, authoritative voice.

"Serving a mission," Jacob said.

I was shocked and amazed. This was truly an eye-opener—not that my eldest son had given the answer I was hoping for, but that he had been asked—twice—what the Lord's chosen servants felt was the most important question: whether he was preparing to serve a mission. Is there a more obvious example of the importance placed upon missionary service? It's clear to me that every young man should be asked the same questions: Are you preparing for a mission? What are you going to be doing in nine years, five years, three years, or perhaps next year?

The time to prepare is now. This is the time to look within your heart and determine for yourself why a mission is so important. When an Apostle of the Lord asks my son, "Are you preparing for a mission?", I envision the Lord asking the same question, for indeed he would. Such questions and counsel can be applied to the older generation, as well. There is a pressing need for greater missionary service, more stalwart determination to live gospel principles, and greater eagerness to share the truth. Perhaps you are of retirement age or have sufficient resources to serve as adult couple missionaries. If you can, in the words of President Spencer W. Kimball, "Just do it!" Whatever your age or circumstances, your blessings will be great as you share the message of the gospel.

A Plea for Forgiveness
A Baby-Sitter's Grief

I'll never forget an evening when my wife and I returned home from a date. It was a late Saturday night, and as we pulled into the driveway we recognized a couple of cars that belonged to some young men from our ward. We thought nothing of it. In whatever city we have lived, our home has often been used as a gathering place for many of the youth.

During our evenings out, there was always a baby-sitter in charge who was given clear instructions on how to handle our five children, when to put them in bed, and what to do about guests. The rule was that as long as things were kept under control and the children abided by their scheduled bedtime, it was okay to have others visit after the children were asleep. It was actually a rare occurrence when a youth would drop by while Patti and I were out for the evening, and I usually didn't mind. But on this occasion I did.

As my wife and I walked to the front door, we found the jacket of a rental movie lying on our front porch. I picked up the cover and began reading. I honestly don't remember the title of the movie but I do remember its rating. "Rated R," the bold letters declared. "Where did this come from?" I asked Patti. She was as dumbfounded as I was. I hesitated to open the front door, fearing that my suspicions of a group of young men in the house watching the movie would be true.

We walked in. Four young men were gathered in the kitchen, drinking juice and eating what was left of a frosted cake.

"Where did this movie come from?" I asked. Caught off guard, the young men turned and looked at each other, each one hoping someone else would speak. I stared intensely at the group, waiting for an answer.

Finally Thomas, the eldest of the group, spoke up. "We rented it because I heard it was a good movie," he said.

"This movie is rated R. There are no R-rated movies allowed in this house," I said. "Each of you knows I would never allow this movie in the house. Why would you rent it, knowing I would disapprove?"

No one spoke a word. A moment of silence passed; it must have felt like an eternity to the young men, who by now had rather sad countenances. The eldest in the bunch spoke again. "We shouldn't have rented it," he said. "We're sorry about that." A couple of the other young men followed his example and apologized. I then strongly reminded them about following the prophet's counsel to not watch R-rated movies, no matter how tame we believe they are. After trying to show forth "an increase of love" (see D&C 121:43) following my rather strong rebuke, we changed the conversation and talked about other events in their lives.

One young man remained relatively quiet during the group's conversation. He was the baby-sitter, Bill, who had allowed the young men into the house, and who I felt was largely responsible for the events of the evening. He knew he was in charge of the household when we were out, and he likely felt a great deal of guilt, knowing that he could and should have prevented the night of movie-watching.

When the young men finally decided to leave, one of them offered Bill a ride home. "Hold on, Bill," I called out. "I want to take you home; we need to talk." I could tell by the expression on Bill's face that he was not looking forward to our little discussion.

As we drove, I reminded Bill of the importance of responsibility, of his charge as a keeper of the house, and of his duty to ensure sanctity in the home. "You were in charge," I said. "I left my home and my family in your care. You should have been the one to speak up and say, 'Wait a minute, guys. I don't want that movie played here.'" I continued, but with a bit more firmness and volume in my voice. "When I ask you to watch the children and the house, I expect you to do as I would do, and ask yourself in every situation if it would be something I would approve of. Do you think for a moment I would have allowed you or anyone else to watch an R-rated movie in our house?"

"No," he said quietly.

He sat and listened attentively as I spoke, but he said nothing. I continued the slow drive to his home, which was now only a block away. It was quiet, and Bill was obviously feeling bad. His head was bowed, his eyes drooped, and his hands were clutched together on top of his knees. Occasionally he would let out a sigh and nervously run both hands through his hair. I wondered whether I had come down too hard on the young man. It was not my intention to make him feel terrible; I just wanted to remind him of his responsibility.

The silence was suddenly broken by a quick sniffle and whimper. I glanced over toward Bill while trying to keep my eyes on the road, and saw him wipe a tear from his cheek. He turned away and looked out the window. There were more sniffles and more wiping tears from his eyes. He was trying to hold back his sobs, but could not. He was visibly heartbroken.

I pulled into Bill's driveway, turned the motor off, looked him in the eyes, and apologized for my strong rebuke. "I didn't mean to make you cry," I said. "I just wanted to remind you of your role as a baby-sitter and the responsibility you have. I'm sorry for coming down so hard on you."

After another moment of silence, he looked at me with a rather sorrowful countenance and said with a broken voice, "I let you down. I'm sorry." By now there were not just a few tears coursing down his cheeks, but many. Through his sobs he said, "I know I shouldn't have allowed the movie in the house. I'm sorry. How can you trust me ever again? I let you down."

What likely added to this young man's genuine grief was the fact that we shared a strong friendship. Bill was one of our most trusted and competent baby-sitters. He often spent time at our home, even when he was not watching the children. He was always extremely responsible, hardworking—someone I called on frequently to help with this or that. Bill was, and still is, a dear friend. Watching him suffer through this experience was not easy for me, either.

His humility and meekness in asking for forgiveness was enough to make me emotional. A lump grew in my throat as I told him, "Don't think you've lost my friendship or love. You haven't. In fact," I said, trying to reassure him, "I love you more now as a friend than I did before."

"Why?" he asked. "Why, after what I did?"

"Because you have a heart that can be touched, and a spirit that recognizes wrong," I explained. "For that I am grateful. I fear for the person who can walk away from an incident like this without the slightest regard for what he did. Only a person with a hard heart could do that."

In my mind, Bill had demonstrated that he recognized his mistake and hated it. He was openly remorseful, blamed no one but himself, and pleaded for forgiveness. I couldn't help but love him for his repentant attitude.

Perhaps, in some extremely small measure, I felt how the Lord must feel when we come to him in deep humility, with broken and contrite hearts. The Lord loves his children; but how much more his love is extended when we recognize our imperfections and cry unto him for forgiveness, pleading for his continuing love and trust. The Lord is merciful, kind, and generous with his love and patience, even though, as the scriptures teach, he "cannot look upon sin with the least degree of allowance" (D&C 1:31).

Bill taught me an important lesson that night about repentance, meekness, submissiveness, and forgiveness. This was not a serious sin he had committed, and it was hardly one anyone would weep over. Even so, this young man, because of his innocent heart, recognized what he had done and felt deep remorse. It was a gentle but powerful reminder to me of what we must all do when we act contrary to the Lord's teachings.

None of us is perfect, and we will never be completely worthy of the Lord's abundant blessings. But we can try; we can plead for his help, guidance, strength, and wisdom. No problem is too small or too large for his attention; but we must take those first steps of recognizing what we have done wrong and striving to make it right. In doing so, we can overcome the many weaknesses in our own lives.

A PROMPTING IGNORED
The Bitter Anguish of Ignoring the Spirit

It was Thanksgiving Day; I remember it well because I had not been called into work. Unlike most professions, my work is dictated by current events, which are no respecters of weekends or special occasions. The news must be printed every day, so having a holiday off is a great cause for celebration. When I look back over my years as a reporter, it's more common to remember holidays spent at the office or in some strange location than those enjoyed at home with the family.

On this particular Thanksgiving Day, I was sitting at home with a couple of families we had invited over, attempting to digest the overabundance of food I had forced myself to eat, when some youth friends, Aaron and Carl, called. (Three-way calling comes in quite handy when trying to plan an event.) Some of the young men in the ward wanted to get together and play hockey later in the evening at one of the roller rinks at a nearby park. My sons and I agreed to join them.

After we ate dessert and lounged around the house long enough for our stomachs to settle, I grabbed my two sons, Jacob and Matthew, and headed off to the park. The outdoor roller rink we played on was a dimly lit, medium-sized rink that was heavily used during hockey season, which in southern Florida seems to be all year. The only reason it was free tonight was because of the holiday.

As we arrived, we noticed two teenage boys playing hockey inside the rink. One of the boys was preparing to leave, but the other wanted to join us, so we included him as we divided into teams. He wasn't a member of the Church, but he quickly came to know a few of the young men who were playing; six or seven youth had come out to skate. We played for nearly two hours, having a terrific time—until we heard the call from a police officer who was standing on a grassy hill overlooking the rink. "Everyone off the rink," he shouted. "The park is closed, and no one is allowed on the rinks. You have ten minutes to leave."

Most of the young men scattered like frightened birds just let out of a cage. A few of us, including myself and our new nonmember friend, stayed in the rink and approached the police officer. I spoke with the officer for a couple of minutes and told him we would clear the rink after picking up our belongings. It was nearly ten o'clock at night, and we had been playing for quite a while, so we didn't mind the interruption. Besides, my body ached from too many falls and checks from my younger, more energetic friends.

I gathered the youth, who by now were making their way back to the rink, and told them we had to leave. As we were removing our roller blades and loading our equipment, I walked up to the young nonmember youth who had joined us on the rink. "You're a pretty good hockey player," I said.

"Huh?" he responded.

"I said you're a good hockey player."

"Oh, thank you," he said.

I noticed, from the few words he spoke, that he had a thick accent and probably didn't speak or understand English very well.

"Tu puedes hablar English?" I asked.

"Si," he said with a big smile, somewhat surprised that I could speak Spanish. Actually, I've never prided myself on my Spanish-speaking ability. When I find myself in foreign countries where Spanish is the native tongue, I can carry out a simple interview, but I hardly know enough to have an intelligent conversation.

As he was sitting alone, removing his hockey pads and skates, I spoke with him in Spanish, asking a few more questions. "So, how old are you?" I inquired.

"Sixteen," he said.

"What's your name?"

"Eduardo Vitaver."

"Do you come and play here very often?"

My small talk was an attempt to get to know this boy, and I felt a distinct impression to befriend him. We talked for a few minutes, told each other good-bye, and I walked to the vehicle where the young men were waiting for a ride home. We decided to meet at my house for more conversation and dessert. Aaron, Carl, Erick, and Tom still had their roller blades on, so they skated the three blocks to my home, while James and Bruno joined me in the van. As we were getting in the vehicle, I noticed Eduardo sitting alone on the grass. I wasn't sure whether he was waiting for a ride or preparing to walk home. At this late hour, I didn't think it would be too safe to walk alone, even in this suburban neighborhood known for its security. "Do you have a ride home?" I asked.

"No, I'm going to walk," he said.

"Are you sure? I could give you a ride home. I don't mind." I felt impressed to insist on giving him a lift. After turning me down a few times, he finally agreed.

We loaded his gear into the van and drove to his home, which was about a mile and a half from the park. On the way I learned he was from Argentina; he had only lived in Florida for a couple of months, and hadn't really gotten to know very many people. I spoke with him briefly about the young men who were playing hockey, explaining that they all belonged to the same church and got together often. Once again I felt a prompting of the Spirit; this time, it was clear that I needed to tell him more about the Church and the youth program. But I didn't; our small talk took a different direction, and soon we were at his home.

I noticed his father waiting for us in the driveway. The guard at the neighborhood security gate must have notified him that I was bringing his son home. As Eduardo gathered his hockey gear, I briefly spoke with his father, again feeling impressed to talk with his dad about the gospel; but I didn't. Instead, our conversation focused on why I was giving his son a ride home, and I failed to change the subject. As I said good night and drove away, I was reminded again of the Spirit's promptings; but once again I ignored them. In fact, even as I drove home, the thought crossed my mind to turn around and invite the family to church. But I didn't.

I turned to James, seated in the back of the van, and invited him to sit in the front seat. "I wanted to tell them about the Church," I confessed. "That family needs to learn about the gospel." James agreed, but we did nothing and continued our drive to my home.

Later that evening, I told my wife about our hockey game and my experience with sixteen-year-old Eduardo, including the promptings to share the gospel with him and my failure to do so. She lovingly reproved me for not being more bold and listening to the Spirit's counsel. I knew in my heart that I had missed a perfect opportunity to share something that was precious to me. *How could I ignore such promptings?* I asked myself. I had felt the Spirit's direction many times that night, but had refused to act. I knew in my heart that the Lord was not pleased.

Time passed, and I completely forgot about that Thanksgiving night. Eight days later, I picked up the morning paper; there, on the front page of the local section, was a picture of the young man I had taken home. *That's Eduardo Vitaver,* I told myself. Then I read the headline next to his picture: "Family of Four Shot Dead."

CRIME SCENE: Detectives and crime technicians investigate at the Weston house where four people were found dead.

JOE RIMKUS JR. / Herald Staff

I couldn't believe it. It felt like a dream. I closed the door to my study, then read the article and wept. Eduardo, his younger sister, and their mother were all shot and killed by their father, who then turned the gun on himself. Friends and family said the father was depressed over his job, their new surroundings, and his failure to find meaning in his move to the United States.

"What have I done?" I cried. "Will the Lord ever forgive me?" I knelt in prayer, grief-stricken over the death of this family and deeply ashamed at having ignored the promptings of the

Weston man kills family, then himself

By CONNIE PILOTO,
JULIE KAY
And JACQUELINE CHARLES
Herald Staff Writers

With the threat of eviction looming, a Weston father turned on his family, fatally shooting his two teenage children and his wife as they had breakfast.

The man, Daniel Eduardo Vitaver, then shot himself in the head, police said.

It was a tragic and startling end to months of financial problems that Vitaver had been battling since moving from Argentina and settling his family on a neat cul-de-sac in the gated community.

Vitaver was drowning in debt, family and friends said. His car payment was due and the rent on the family's four-bedroom, house on Cascade Falls Drive was two months in arrears.

Things were so bad that Vitaver's teenage son could not afford

lunch at McDonald's. He could not go to the movies. He could not play at arcades. The boy tearfully confided the family's secret to his best friend.

"His father was having bad money problems," said William Cunha, 14, Eduardo's best friend. "He was crying. His father couldn't afford anything."

The Broward Sheriff's Office said the pressure apparently became too much for the medical technology sales representative.

Vitaver, 53, was found lying face-down in a pool of blood, one hand across his chest. The revolver used to kill his wife, Magalia Regina Vitaver, 49, and their children, 19-year-old Cynthia and 16-year-old Eduardo, was found in the other.

A time of death had not been established, but police suspect the

PLEASE SEE FAMILY, 23A

Spirit. I had full knowledge of my guilt, and was suffering the bitter misery of a lost soul. I cried and pleaded with the Lord for his forgiveness.

There have been only a few times in my life when I have felt such a tremendous burden of guilt and pain, and this was clearly one of them. Even at this writing, my eyes grow wet with tears over what I was clearly prompted to do, yet failed to do. My heart aches, knowing that I may someday be held accountable for ignoring the repeated whisperings of the Spirit and neglecting my responsibilities as a member of the Church.

Thanksgiving night all seemed to make so much sense to me now: the promptings to befriend the boy; my insistence on giving him a ride home; our discussion about friends; meeting and spending a moment with his father; and above all, hearing the powerful promptings of the Spirit. *Could the gospel have made a difference in their lives?* I asked myself, trying to justify my inaction. I quickly realized I was asking a question I already knew the answer to. Of *course* it could have made a difference. The true gospel, if accepted, always makes a difference in an individual's life. It is the difference between eternal salvation and spiritual death. Is it any wonder, then, that every member of the Church is urged to share the gospel with friends and neighbors? As President George Albert Smith counseled, "Each of us has a responsibility to share [the gospel] with others... so let us not lose our opportunity, let us not lose the privilege that the Lord has given to us to teach his truth" (Conference address, 1950).

Since my experience with Eduardo and his family, the significance of this counsel has had a much more powerful impact upon me. Sharing the gospel is a responsibility and a privilege that we must all shoulder; if it is ignored, we have been told through modern-day revelation that we could be held accountable for the lives of those we might have saved. They are lives like those still embedded in my mind today: the faces of sixteen-year-old Eduardo and his father.

Part Four

"Counsel with the Lord in All Thy Doings, and He Will Direct Thee for Good" (Alma 37:37)

No greater peace, no greater solace, no greater wisdom can be found than on bended knee in open supplication to God.

"Counsel with the Lord in All Thy Doings, and He Will Direct Thee for Good"

FOREWORD

President Howard W. Hunter, fourteenth president of The Church of Jesus Christ of Latter-day Saints, once wrote, "If we look to man and the ways of the world, we will find turmoil and confusion. If we look to God, we will find peace for the restless soul" (Howard W. Hunter, *That We Might Have Joy* [Salt Lake City: Deseret Book Company, 1994], p. 27).

One cannot speak enough about prayer. It is the conduit by which peace, strength, direction, and happiness come. Prayer has always been a powerful part of life for me and my family. We gather in the morning, kneeling around our living room table, to extend our thanks to God for a new day. At mealtimes, we thank the Lord for the food he has provided and pray that we might be generous enough to help those in need. In the evening, we give thanks for another day's protection and guidance, and pray the Lord's blessings upon our prophet and others called of God to lead us.

Admittedly, it's not always convenient to gather for family prayer. I have often caught myself, late at night after a family outing or church gathering, telling our children, "Okay, it's really late . . . time to jump into bed." Inevitably, one of the children will say, "But, Dad, we haven't read the scriptures or said family prayer yet." My heart sinks. Again I have been reminded by a young child of the importance of prayer and scripture reading. What a blessing these children are to me! Not only do they bring joy and happiness into my life, but inspiration as well. They are much closer to their Father in Heaven than we will ever know.

Because prayer is of such great worth and importance to our family, we have devised a regular practice that allows us to have family prayer when I'm traveling. (I'm usually on the road about five months out of the year.) In the study of our home sits a speaker phone; and through the wonder of cellular phone technology, we have morning and evening conference calls and family prayer.

When I'm on the road, every morning before the children head off to school and every evening before they go to sleep, they call my pager number. If I'm in a location where there is no pager service, I'll call in at designated times—usually sometime before 7:00 in the morning or 8:45 in the evening. This gives me an opportunity to talk about the day's events, speak with my wife and children individually, and of course, kneel with them for family prayer. The practice has been most rewarding, even though I'll admit that it hasn't always been convenient to call. In fact, sometimes it's been a great inconvenience. I might be in a time zone several hours earlier than the one at home, so I'm paged and awakened at 3:00 in the morning. I could be in the middle of a remote village in a foreign land, preparing to conduct an interview, but I'll call in at the designated times. Of course, there are days when circumstances don't permit me to make the call during our standard morning and evening conferences. When I know it's going to be a problem, I'll call in much earlier to leave a lengthy message on the answering machine, ending with a request for someone to offer a prayer. The message is then played back during the morning or evening gathering.

I've placed calls from some pretty strange locations. I recall sitting in a military truck, surrounded by Mexican troops, racing off to cover a drug war in central Mexico. I remember calling from Managua, Nicaragua, during one of the presidential election rallies, holding the phone high in the air and telling the children, "Listen to the voices of 100,000 cheering people, yelling and screaming for a candidate!" I've called from villages in Haiti, describing in detail the squalid conditions of the impoverished country. My calls have come from the riot-torn streets of Los Angeles and from 57th Street in Manhattan. From a hurricane-ravaged city on the East Coast to the rainy city of Seattle. From a boat on the Florida Bay to the courtrooms of many of this nation's most notorious criminal trials. From the Camp Davidian

Compound siege in Waco, Texas, to the hostage crisis in Lima, Peru. From a tornado-torn town in the Southeast, to the central plains of the Midwest, and from tragic air disasters from South America to the Caribbean. At least the children get a feel for what I'm doing, and perhaps they're learning something about the world.

I've called from planes, trains, taxis, buses, and believe it or not, donkeys, horses, boats, and just about anything that moves. It's always a joy to see the reaction of someone near me when I ask one of the children to offer prayer. I suddenly turn silent, bow my head and close my eyes, then later speak the word, "Amen!" Those who frequently travel with me aren't so surprised by my morning and evening conference calls. In fact, they count on them. When I'm paged at the usual evening hour, the response from some of my colleagues is the same. "Oh, it's the Rascon children," they'll say as I leave the restaurant table for our evening family conference call. Then, "How's the family doing?" they ask upon my return. I proceed to tell them about every one of the children. Soon they are sorry they asked.

Although there are times when making the call is inconvenient, I wouldn't trade the experience for anything in the world. I have learned a great truth through family prayer by phone. No matter what the location, no matter how busy the world around us, or what troubling thought is piercing the mind, when I have the phone to my ear, listening to the prayerful voice of one of my children or my dear wife, a great peace comes over me. I am suddenly filled, when only moments earlier I was empty. The day may be hectic and contentious, boisterous or unnerving, but when I pause for that moment of prayer, there is a bit of the sweetness of heaven. The morning or evening just doesn't feel the same if circumstances don't permit us to have that special contact.

It is truly a sobering thought to think that some individuals go through life without prayer. I couldn't imagine it. Like food that provides sustenance for the body, prayer provides energy for the soul and spirit. Prayer is the vehicle of light and inspiration that allows us access to the heavens. Without it, we are left to the uninspired teachings of men, directed only by the human mind. What a terrible, terrible loss it is to be separated from God by an inability or unwillingness to pray.

If this chapter provides any measure of motivation or inspiration to make prayer a daily part of life, I will consider this entire work completely justified. It's that important! I am reminded of one of my favorite hymns:

> *Ere you left your room this morning,*
> *Did you think to pray?*
> *In the name of Christ, our Savior,*
> *Did you sue for loving favor*
> *As a shield today?*
>
> *When your heart was filled with anger,*
> *Did you think to pray?*
> *Did you plead for grace, my brother,*
> *That you might forgive another*
> *Who had crossed your way?*
>
> *When sore trials came upon you,*
> *Did you think to pray?*
> *When your soul was full of sorrow,*
> *Balm of Gilead did you borrow*
> *At the gates of day?*

And the chorus:

> *Oh, how praying rests the weary!*
> *Prayer will change the night to day.*
> *So, when life gets dark and dreary,*
> *Don't forget to pray.* (Hymns, No. 140)

PRAYER FROM THE SKY
A Wild Ride on a Single-Engine Plane

Frequently in my travels, I fly chartered jets or planes. I generally fly them only when there is a breaking news story, when it's imperative to get to the location quickly and there are no commercial airlines available.

One particularly busy hurricane season, after filing my morning reports and leaving the scene of a hurricane, I was told to return to the site by chartered aircraft. I had finished a live morning news report for the national *CBS This Morning* show, and was told by New York that because there was no serious damage related to this storm, they would not be running an evening news piece. The passing hurricane was a powerful one, but not strong enough to do a tremendous amount of damage. There was, however, a torrential downpour from the storm, and winds forceful enough to close schools, most businesses, and all the airports in the region. After gathering my belongings, I jumped in my vehicle and began driving south, away from the storm, toward the nearest airport that was open.

About mid-afternoon, the New York office paged me and told me to get to the nearest airport, where there would be charter plane waiting to fly me back up north to cover a breaking news story related to the hurricane. High winds from the storm had created fifteen-foot sea swells that had capsized a small tourist pleasure boat off the coast of northern Florida. Everyone had been thrown overboard. I was told that the United States Coast Guard was already at the site and had participated in some dramatic helicopter rescues that were caught on tape by a Coast Guard photographer.

The closest airport was in West Palm Beach; as I made my way there, my Miami office made a desperate search for an aircraft and pilot to fly me north. Because of the storm, the search wasn't easy. Initially there were no willing pilots, but after an exhaustive search, a hesitant but agreeable soul was found. Naturally, I wasn't completely comfortable with the situation. First of all, I couldn't imagine why anyone would be willing to fly under these rather extreme weather conditions and place himself, his passengers, and the aircraft in harm's way. Also unsettling was the fact that my office was not able to find a Lear jet, which could fly in much more severe weather conditions than a propelled plane. The pilot they found was an elderly gentleman who likely didn't realize what he was getting himself into—and his copilot was a fifteen-year-old boy! I knew we would be flying into the midst of a hurricane, but did the pilot truly understand this? I didn't think so. The situation seemed to go from bad to worse.

I jumped into the small prop plane. We taxied down the runway and had a pleasant, uneventful liftoff. It was a nice start. The further we flew north, however, the more bumpy it became. I looked outside my small window; it was visibly stormy, and I could literally see the darkness ahead, the dense cloud configurations, and the rain that had begun pounding the front windshield. Not surprisingly, the wind and rain grew progressively worse the farther we flew north.

There was no question that the weather was not the best for flying. In fact, it was horrible. It was no great wonder that every other pilot CBS News had contacted refused to fly. Then again, perhaps this elderly pilot knew what he was doing. I had my doubts, however. I've flown in everything from hot air balloons to fighter jets, from makeshift homemade contraptions to bomber planes, so I've become somewhat familiar with the flying limitations and capabilities of a variety of aircraft in various weather conditions. Even so, I decided to give my pilot the benefit of the doubt, and trust in his experience and judgment.

As our journey took us farther north, serious concerns about what I was doing began to set in. The weather grew progressively worse, and the ride was getting extremely violent. I was literally being bounced up and down like a basketball. I stretched forward to get a better look at the pilot. He was fiddling with the radio system, trying to get in contact with ground control. On his lap was a large pilot's map of directions and airports, and his youthful copilot was trying to point to various locations. I was sure we were lost; at least my pilots gave me every reason to believe we were. *This doesn't look good,* I quietly told myself.

By now, the ride was the worst I had ever felt on a plane. We were making drops and sharp climbs so ferociously that when I looked out the window, the wings of the small aircraft appeared to be flapping like a bird's. The bounce was terrible. I tightened my seat belt and looked at the pilot. "Are we going to be all right?" I asked. "It's getting pretty rough up here."

"It's bad," he responded. "The weather is worse than I thought. I don't know how long the plane can take this." This was not a reassuring comment, and it was my first clue that the pilot was as concerned as I was. I began to wonder why I had ever decided to take this flight, knowing that we would be faced with violent weather.

"How much farther to the Melbourne Airport?" I asked, taking long breaths between words to make up for the wild turbulence.

"I think it's about fifteen minutes or so," the pilot muttered. And in a much softer tone, "But I'm not sure…we have no communication with the tower."

Well, I thought, *here I am in one of the most unstable aircrafts in the sky, flying through the edges of a hurricane in near darkness, searching for an airport that my pilot has no communication with.* Prospects for a safe landing did not look good.

At this point I was quite nervous, but not fearing for my life. Still, I leaned back in my seat and began to think about my existence—about my children and my dear wife, about my friends and brothers and sisters. It was during this rather pensive moment that an update came from the pilot. "I think the airport is over here," he said, "but the control tower has been evacuated, the airport is closed, and the wind has apparently knocked out electrical power for runway lights."

This was a small airport, so the news didn't surprise me, although it was certainly not reassuring. What followed was even less comforting. "Hold on to your seat," the pilot said. "We're going to try a visual approach landing on the runway."

Holding on didn't do much good on that plane. The wind and rain were buffeting us around like a bird without wings in a wild windstorm. We were at the mercy of nature's elements, which by now were so powerful and fierce that visibility must have been less than twenty-five feet. It was late afternoon, and the sky was darkened by storm clouds that caused a thick blackness to cover the sky. And because the storm had knocked out electricity in the city, there were no lights anywhere.

We began the gradual decent for our visual approach. I could see the pilot concentrating on his instruments as he periodically glanced out the front windshield. Would the runway be there when we touched down? I watched the control panel as our altitude dropped. I nervously squeezed the arms of my seat, noticing that the pilot held a tight grip on the controls with each hand. He appeared transfixed. With one word, I knew there were problems with our visual approach.

"Trees!" the pilot yelled. "Trees!" He quickly yanked the controls toward him, and we began a sharp ascent. I'm not sure how far the runway was from us, but we missed the trees by what seemed like only several feet.

"I have to land this plane," the pilot cried in a frightened voice. He wasn't looking at me or the copilot when he called out; he was making an obvious assessment of our problem, and the solution was clear in his mind. It was clear in mine, too.

"We have to get this plane down, NOW!" he yelled even louder. I wasn't about to argue. I wanted to get the plane down, too!

"I'll try it again. I'll try another approach," he said with a disturbing tone of uncertainty and nervousness in his voice. It was obvious that he, too, was visibly shaken by this wild ride; you could see it in his facial expression and in his tight, sweaty grip on the controls. Meanwhile, his young copilot sat staring out the window, seemingly mesmerized by what was undoubtedly his first jolting experience in the single-engine plane. His hands held firmly to his shoulder belt, and his feet and legs were firmly planted on the floor of the plane.

By now I was beginning to get nervous. For the first time I could remember, I was genuinely afraid that we would have to make a crash landing, and the possibility of losing my life was very real. Thoughts began to race through my mind, and again I thought of my wife and children, my parents, friends, brothers, and sisters. Then I thought of prayer. *Where else can I find help and peace?* I said to myself. *Who better to ask for guidance and comfort than the One who created the wind and the rain? The Lord knows all things. It is He I should request a blessing from and in behalf of our pilots.*

So there, in the middle of the sky, while we continued to bounce uncontrollably, I bowed my head, closed my eyes, and offered a prayer. A prayer from the sky. In part, I said, "Dear Father…if it be thy will, wilt thou please direct this pilot. Wilt thou grant us a safe landing and a break in weather conditions."

Upon finishing my prayer, I immediately felt a calming sensation come over me. A great peace filled my heart, and I felt the Spirit of the Lord close to me. I was assured, through the whisperings and comforting guidance of the Holy Ghost, that all would be well, that we would land safely, and that no lives would be lost. The promptings were so strong that I had no doubt they were true. No matter what occurred, I knew we would be safe. I tightened my seat belt one more time and calmly leaned back in my seat.

The pilot was once again staring out the front window, frantically searching for the runway. His head was moving back and forth as we made our second visual approach, and his actions told me he was more lost now than during our first approach. Our descent was fast and wild, but seemed to be going well until I heard the words, "Trees! More trees!" I didn't flinch at his words as I did before. I knew in my heart that we would all land safely. Again he yanked the controls back and we quickly lifted, bouncing as our altitude climbed. "We need to get this plane down. The weather is not getting better," he said, sounding out of breath and extremely tense.

"Why don't we just search for a clearing and land anywhere," I suggested. The pilot agreed. He took the controls with one hand, and with the other started pointing to various positions on the map. His copilot finally started to loosen up, and he tried to help.

"I think there's a field over here," the pilot said, pointing to the right of the aircraft. He began turning the plane in that direction. Within minutes the clouds cleared, there was a break in the rain, and the sun shone through on an open field. We made one pass to ensure that it looked safe and clear enough to land.

Moments later, we landed in that open field. It was a bit rough and bumpy, but completely safe. All was well, as promised by the Lord. This was another testament to the power of prayer, another witness of the Lord's love for his children, and another example of God's answer to a frightened cry from one of his own.

The experience was powerful. I was once again reminded that we are not forgotten or left alone in this dangerous and unpredictable world. We have a Father in Heaven who loves us and knows our individual needs. We have a loving brother, the Lord Jesus Christ, who intercedes in our behalf, and we have the Holy Ghost to prompt us and grant us knowledge, direction, and enlightenment. Prayer is true rest for the troubled heart; it is the avenue by which the Lord's children can communicate with him at any time, in any place, under any circumstances or conditions. How grateful I am for this reassuring lifeline to heaven!

"Arthur, Did You Say Your Prayers?"

Memories of Ricks College

I attended Ricks College in Rexburg, Idaho, during 1980 and '81. What a terrific experience it was! I had a wonderful time, and graduated feeling as though I had taken advantage of every opportunity to broaden my education, enlighten my spiritual understanding, and hone my journalistic skills. I believe one of the reasons my time at Ricks was so eventful was that I kept myself extremely busy. I was overloaded with eighteen to twenty credits each semester, held a job that required me to work nearly forty hours a week, and managed a campus radio station that required another ten hours a week.

From the time I entered college in the fall of 1980, my schedule, like those of so many other students, was overwhelmingly hectic. I had little time for social activities, rarely dated, and found myself spending most of my time alone. But I loved what I was doing and knew, even then, that I was gaining tremendous practical experience at work and an excellent education at school.

My classes would start at seven or eight in the morning and end early in the afternoon. I would then head to my office in one of the buildings on campus and take care of responsibilities at the college radio stations, KVIK and KRIC. Because I was a student manager of one of the radio stations, I was given an office, which came in quite handy when I needed some quiet time and a place to do homework. I would usually finish my work at the radio stations by five o'clock, which gave me just enough time to eat dinner at the campus cafeteria and drive to KRXK, the commercial AM radio station in Rexburg.

I started working at KRXK in January of 1981 as a disc jockey and news reader. The shift was from six to midnight, six nights a week. By the time I returned to my apartment at 12:30 in the morning, I was exhausted. If there was homework I hadn't completed, this early morning hour was the only time to do it.

During this chaotic time, I became so focused on my studies and work at the radio stations that I began to lose sight of the truly important areas of life. Don't misunderstand; I was never a bad kid, but I was beginning to ignore the little things that, over time, make a big difference in one's spirituality. For example, my regular scripture reading gradually turned into a weekly instead of daily occurrence, and my morning and evening prayers became only occasional. My church attendance was regular, but I didn't have a calling and felt like I was drifting. Many times I had to leave church meetings early because of my work schedule at KRXK, and I rarely attended family home evening gatherings due to my work at the radio station.

Overall, my association with the Church was growing distant. Of course, I always knew in my heart that the Church was true, and I never lost sight of my desire to serve a faithful mission. I was aware of what needed to be done to strengthen my spiritual growth and activity; but I was a young eighteen-year-old, excited about laying the groundwork of my career, and I just didn't stop to realize what was happening.

At the end of the 1981 summer session, the apartment I was living in underwent a few changes. A couple of students in the six-person apartment moved out, two others moved in, and I moved into a different room. My new roommate had lived in the apartment most of the summer, but I had never really gotten to know him; in fact, even now I can't remember his name. But I'll never forget his face, his gentle words, and the influence he had on my life.

When the fall semester began, I found myself so overloaded with work and school that I spent very little time at the apartment. I was there usually between the hours of midnight and seven in the morning. My association with my new roommate consisted of a "good night" when I walked into the room past midnight, and a "good morning" when I would occasionally see him before I left the apartment. But even with this limited association, I later learned that my roommate watched me much more closely than I realized, and was genuinely concerned for my spiritual well-being. He loved me, and I felt that love through his example and by the way he treated me. Although we rarely spoke to each other, he was the single person reminding me to get ready for church, attend firesides and devotionals, read the scriptures, and say my prayers.

As I look back on that period of my life, I would be remiss if I didn't recognize my roommate's unique but powerful way of influencing my life. The lessons he inadvertently taught, and those I most vividly remember, occurred late at night. They began when I would walk into our bedroom and find him kneeling in prayer.

The next lessons were more direct. One evening, as I was climbing into bed, he surprised me with a question. "Arthur," he said, sounding like my mother after I'd done something she didn't approve of.

"What?" I said, surprised that he was even awake. It was dark enough so I couldn't see his bed on the other side of the room.

"Arthur, did you say your prayers?" he would ask in a soft, polite voice.

The first time he asked me this question, I honestly didn't know what to say. I suppose I was shocked, more than anything else. *What is he doing, asking me if I said my prayers?* I thought. I considered saying "yes," just to end the conversation quickly. Instead, I simply told him the truth.

"Uh, no...I'm too tired."

He didn't say anything after that, and neither did I. I lay down, staring into the darkness, thinking about the last time I had said my evening prayers. I was sure it had been a few days. *Who does he think he is, asking me if I said my prayers?* I thought as I rolled over and went to sleep.

A couple of nights later, once again as I was climbing into bed, a soft voice came from the other side of the room. "Arthur, I didn't see you saying your prayers."

This time I didn't say anything; I just jumped into bed and tried to go to sleep. But I found myself thinking about his persistence. My roommate always seemed happy, content, and spiritually secure. He was a returned missionary, and would occasionally share with me experiences he'd had during his service. There was a goodness about him that I recognized and admired.

Several nights passed before the next reminder. "Arthur," came the serene voice from his side of the room. "It's important to say your prayers."

Over time, I learned to just mumble a few words to my roommate; perhaps he would think I was saying my prayers. But I clearly remember thinking to myself, *Who is this guy? I can't believe he keeps asking me these questions.* Sometimes I wouldn't enter the room until after I thought he was asleep, but that didn't work, either. There were times when he would even ask me to kneel beside him in prayer.

Finally, the night came when I gave in to his kind, gentle pleadings. By this time, my own conscience had been pricked, and I couldn't go on ignoring his near-nightly calls.

"Arthur," came his ever constant and sincere, familiar voice. "Did you remember to say your prayers? Your Father in Heaven would like to hear from you."

I couldn't believe it. "Okay," I said rather impatiently, "I'll say my prayers!"

For the first time in a long time, I knelt and prayed. My own guilt—and, I might add, the relentless promptings of my roommate—had finally brought me to my knees. But over time, as the reminders and my prayers became more frequent, I began to realize how much I needed the Lord and missed the direction of his holy spirit.

I discovered that what I truly yearned for could not be found through academic or professional achievement, but only through kneeling in humility and faith, with an open heart toward God. Through prayer I found true peace and solace, and as time passed I became more aware of spiritual matters and developed a brighter attitude about myself and the Church. My work at the radio stations actually improved, and it wasn't long until I began preparing more diligently for my mission.

I am reminded of a favorite hymn of mine, written by LDS author Emma Lou Thayne. Its title echoes a resounding question that nearly everyone has likely asked: "Where Can I Turn for Peace?" The song answers in a beautifully scripted poem that any humble seeker of peace will appreciate.

The first verse, a cry for comfort, we often silently repeat in our hearts:

> *Where can I turn for peace?*
> *Where is my solace*
> *When other sources seek to make me whole?*
> *When with a wounded heart, anger, or malice,*
> *I draw myself apart,*
> *Searching my soul?*

With the second verse comes a realization of where that comfort can be found:

> *Where, when my aching grows,*
> *Where, when I languish,*
> *Where, in my need to know, where can I run?*
> *Where is the quiet hand to calm my anguish?*
> *Who, who can understand?*
> *He, only One.*

And finally, the Lord's answer to our distress is a personal manifestation of his love:

> *He answers privately,*
> *Reaches my reaching*
> *In my Gethsemane,*
> *Savior and Friend.*
> *Gentle the peace he finds for my beseeching.*
> *Constant he is and kind,*
> *Love without end.* (Hymns, No. 129)

Is there a more beautiful message of hope for one who seeks solace? For one with a troubled heart? Christ is truly our "Savior and Friend," to whom we can confidently look as we ask, "Where can I turn for peace?".

The world has no power to bring us comfort or peace. Education, a professional career, or the wisdom of men and women will never satisfy our longings for spiritual fulfillment. But all who call upon the Savior will receive his gentle peace and constant, reassuring love. As the poetic verse so poignantly declares, "Who, who can understand? He, only One."

"GRAT GWENTA HIGH MAN, BORN 1586"
A Prayer Answered in Oklahoma City

When I look back on some of my most memorable experiences with prayer, I can't help thinking of Oklahoma City and the bombing of the Federal Building. The city was living a nightmare, and prayer seemed to give the people a great deal of strength. I, too, shared in this blessing.

It was a difficult couple of weeks in Oklahoma City, covering such an emotional and heartbreaking disaster. The work was endless, the days long and hard. After nearly two weeks, I was tired and worn. My schedule kept me busy from four-thirty in the morning until seven or eight o'clock at night. It was a grueling schedule without any days off, and the terrible nature of the story added to my exhaustion of body and spirit. More than 160 people were killed in this country's most horrific act of terrorism. Every day more bodies were removed from the rubble while family, friends, and loved ones gathered, hoping beyond hope that someone would be found alive. Every day I found myself dealing with death and misery, sorrow and sadness, anger and anguish. It was physically, emotionally, and spiritually draining.

On a certain Thursday evening, after I had finished my work for the CBS morning and evening news programs, I returned to our makeshift office for a rather informal meeting. This hastily assembled office near downtown Oklahoma City was where correspondents, producers, editors, photographers, sound technicians, engineers, and New York management orchestrated news coverage for CBS. That, in itself, was quite a sight. It always amazed me to see the number of resources CBS would bring to cover a major news event. The resources only seemed to double when Dan Rather was anchoring from the scene, as he was during the coverage of the Oklahoma City bombing.

At the meeting, we learned that CBS would be scaling down its resources and allowing most workers to return home. After two weeks of relentless coverage of the disaster, this news did not surprise us. Even Dan Rather would return to New York after Friday's broadcast, and only a skeleton crew—one correspondent, two camera crews, a couple of producers, and a video editor—would remain in Oklahoma City. I was the correspondent who would stay a few more days to cover weekend news and Monday morning's broadcast. I was also told that after filing live reports for the *CBS This Morning* show, I would be free to take the rest of Friday off.

I returned to my hotel that evening, wondering what I could possibly do for an entire day in Oklahoma City. As beautiful as the nation's heartland is, I had no desire to spend my free time in a city where I had worked fifteen hours a day for two nearly weeks. As I was pondering this, several options crossed my mind. I could sleep the day away, or perhaps just relax, read, and catch up on my journal writing. Later that evening, as I read the scriptures and offered my nightly prayers, I asked the Lord for guidance in helping me spend my leisure time productively. Then the answer came; it was as clear to me as this writing is to you. I would ask permission to leave the city, go to Dallas, and attend the temple. Dallas is some two hundred miles south of Oklahoma City, about a three-hour drive or a forty-five-minute flight. I was sure it was what the Lord would have me do.

Allowing faith and optimism to take over, I made reservations on a 9:48 a.m. flight out of Oklahoma City for Friday morning, all the while praying that my executive producers would permit me to make the trip. Surprisingly, they did. In retrospect, I suppose there was no need to marvel over their decision. I was certain the temple was where the Lord wanted me to spend my day; with that assurance, I should have had more faith that my superiors would grant my request.

I finished my duties with the national broadcast that Friday morning. Then I headed directly to the airport, caught a commuter plane to Dallas, and flagged down a taxi. "Where you go, young man?" the driver asked with a heavy accent.

"To the Mormon temple off Preston Street," I told him, unsure whether he had any idea of what I was talking about.

"Oh," he said, "I think I see that building once. Does it have big spirals on top with..." He paused, then blurted out, "....maybe a horn on one of them?"

"That's it," I said. "Could you please take me there?"

As we drove to the temple site, I asked myself a simple question: *Why did I feel so impressed to come to the temple?* I reached in my travel bag and pulled out a Book of Mormon.

"Have you heard of The Church of Jesus Christ of Latter-day Saints?" I asked the driver.

"No, no, no," he said.

"How about the Mormon Church?" I said.

"Oh, Mormons," he said. "Mormons, yes. I know that church."

I began to explain a little about the Church to my friendly driver and presented him with a Book of Mormon. I marked several passages by folding the corner pages, then gathered up my small shoulder bag. "You be sure and read this book, okay?"

"Oh, sure, young man," he said. "I read your book."

I always enjoyed it when someone referred to me as a "young man." Believe me, it rarely happens. The man promised he would read the book, and even agreed to attend a Mormon church in his neighborhood.

Arriving at my destination, I wished the driver farewell and made my way to the front desk of the Dallas Temple. I'll never forget the words of the gentleman who welcomed me to the temple that day. "You come to us from a long distance," he said softly. "I'm sure you'll have a wonderful experience serving in the temple today." This warm greeting set a reverent tone for a day that would be a most fitting conclusion to covering the deadliest act of violence in America. I was scarcely through the front door, and my heart and soul were already filled with deep emotions. The presence of the Lord's spirit was unmistakable.

After changing into my temple clothing, I made my way to the chapel to await the beginning of the session. There I was approached by a sweet, elderly woman. "Excuse me, sir," she said, "I'm one of the temple matrons. When I saw you walking to the chapel, I knew you were the one I was waiting for." She went on. "The Spirit prompted me to ask if you wouldn't mind going through the temple for a certain name we have been holding in the family file section."

"Sure," I said. I wasn't about to disagree with a prompting of the Spirit. She walked back to the counter and pulled out a file card with a few markings on it.

"Here is the name of a man born in 1586. He was believed to be a great Indian chief," she said. "We have been saving the name, waiting for the right person to perform the work. I believe you are that person." She spoke in such a sweet, soft manner and looked like an angel in white who had come to deliver an important message. She smiled and handed me the card.

"I would be honored to perform the work," I told her, then silently asked myself, *Why me? Who am I to be blessed with such an honor as this?*

She smiled and clasped both her hands around mine. "Thank you," she said. "Thank you, and have a wonderful temple session."

She turned and walked away. I stood there briefly, enjoying the spirit of that wonderful moment, then slowly made my way into the chapel. I felt a deep sense of peace and comfort as I walked in. The strong presence of the Spirit of the Lord was unmistakable. Later, I recorded in my journal:

April 28, 1995

I sat down and listened to the beautiful music from the organ. It brought peace to my heart and filled me with an immeasurable amount of joy. I took the card I was given by the sweet temple worker and opened it. The name read, "Grat Gwenta High Man, born 1586." A chilling sensation surrounded my frame, and I felt wrapped in the arms of this man for whom I was to perform an endowment. He was glad I was there. I was glad I was there. I knew without any doubt that this man I was doing proxy work for was rejoicing. I felt a small measure of his joy. After centuries of waiting, he would this day receive the proper ordinances that would prepare him for exaltation. What joy filled my heart. I could not stop the tears from flowing. I pondered the great mission of performing work for those who have passed on. The Lord opened my understanding of this great work, and I felt the presence of many spirits in the temple, as the truthfulness of these temple ordinances was confirmed to me once again.

Suddenly my thoughts drifted back to Oklahoma City, where so many continue to grieve. I couldn't help but mourn their great loss. Pictures vividly passed before me of the many images of disaster and sorrow. Mothers crying for their children. Fathers sobbing for the loss of their wives. Caskets being carried from funeral homes. And the most vivid of all images, the Federal Building and its open shell...this immense concrete tomb that has told all the world that hate is alive in America. The contrast was overwhelming. Here I sit in the house of the Lord, where peace, tranquility, and reverence are paramount, and not far away, where I was reporting from earlier this day, the most blatant example of how evil people can become.

I finished the temple session that day and sat in the celestial room for some time. I had no desire to leave the peace of the temple and face a world filled with ignorance and sin. My time at the temple was too beautiful, and the Spirit's generous gifts too great to desire anything but the quiet, comforting solitude the celestial room provided. Soon enough I had to leave the room; but I took advantage of my time at the temple and went through another session, once again enjoying the blessing of peace and contentment the temple provided.

It was late afternoon before I left the temple. I called a taxi and headed back to the airport, quiet and pensive over the day's events. It was nearly eight o'clock by the time I returned to Oklahoma City. Had time passed so quickly? I felt weak and exhausted. The Spirit had taken much out of me that day. When I knelt in prayer that evening, I thanked the Lord for his love, for the generous outpouring of his spirit to such an unworthy soul as I, and for the promptings from the Spirit to spend my day at the temple. I was blessed beyond measure. Truly, a veil had been lifted from my eyes and replaced with a clearer understanding of the spirits who desperately waited for sacred ordinances to be performed. I gained a new appreciation for the temple from this visit. I understood more deeply the Lord's great plan of salvation, and the tremendous importance these magnificent buildings play in the lives of every man, woman, and child. The tragic and deadly news event I was covering had only added to the depth of my emotions, and had perhaps prepared me for the things I experienced in the temple.

The following day, when I returned to the daily rigors and unpleasantness of the world, I couldn't help pondering how wonderful the world would be if every inhabitant could enjoy what I had experienced only a day earlier. I reflected on how much better the grieving woman I interviewed would deal with the loss of her child; how much better the man would be able to console his children as they faced the death of their mother; how much more faith and comfort all mourners would have if they understood that death is not an end, but a beginning. With great humility, I realized that the celestial world I had savored only the day before was one that members of the Church could and should enjoy on a regular basis. As Latter-day Saints, we *can* enjoy heaven on earth! May we go often to the house of the Lord and partake of its blessings.

DID YOU THINK TO PRAY?
Advice to a Colleague

Some time ago, I was eating dinner with a colleague when we got into a religious discussion. We talked about the LDS faith, his Jewish faith (which he rarely practiced), and other organized religions. We often found ourselves getting into these discussions. You see, my colleague was a philosophical man who enjoyed exploring the mysteries but lacked the faith to believe much of anything. In fact, to him, nothing existed unless one of the senses acknowledged it. He was like the doubting apostle Thomas, to whom seeing was believing.

As our discussion continued, we began talking about his family—specifically, his relationship with his wife. It was for this reason that we were eating this meal together. He had asked me earlier in the day if I would join him for a private dinner. Naturally, I agreed. He told me he had a personal matter to discuss, and because he knew me to be a religious family man, he thought I could be of help. I have learned over time that living the gospel brings many opportunities, and clearly one of those is lending advice to friends and colleagues who recognize your religious convictions and feel of your generous love. They want to experience that same comforting spirit of assurance about life that they have identified in you. Refusing to offer what the Lord has so freely given may perhaps be a sin of omission.

After completing the day's work and filing my report, we found a secluded table at an Italian restaurant. He immediately opened up and spoke plainly. "My wife doesn't love me," he said. "She wants to leave me, but I want to work things out." He went on to explain how their relationship had been difficult at best over the past couple of years, and any attempt at reconciling their differences was not working. It was obvious that he was extremely troubled over the relationship; he was prepared to call it quits, give up, and walk away. What prevented him from doing so were his chil-

dren. He loved them, and he knew a separation would be too difficult a trial for them. He truly was, and still is, a caring, loving
man; yet he sounded hopeless and beaten, lost in a world that to
him offered little more than questions without answers.

"We've been to counselors, we've talked to philosophers, we've
read books about marriage, we've talked to our rabbi, we've done
everything we can possibly do to save this marriage," he continued.
He was confused; he didn't know what else he could do, and had
no idea where he could turn. "We've spent lots of money on people
we thought could help, and nothing has worked." He had even
met with a leading religious figure in his community, but "his
advice was less than satisfactory."

With a bewildered, desperate look on his face, he looked me in
the eyes for a moment and said, "Art, you're a religious man. You
always seem happy and so sure of what this world is all about.
What should I do? What advice do you have for me?"

Who was I, I thought, that I should be asked such a question
by this man, who was several years my senior? What was I to tell
him? It sounded as though he had done nearly everything to save
his marriage. He had sacrificed a great deal of money, time, and
energy to try and make things work. He was frustrated, he said,
that his wife wasn't making much of an effort to compromise, and
he described her attempts as feeble at best.

I thought about his question for what seemed like several
minutes, but I'm confident it was only seconds. He said nothing,
but looked at me, waiting for some profound answer. I said a quick
prayer, asking for direction. After my pause, I felt impressed to ask
my colleague this: "Have you ever knelt down and prayed to God
for help?" My question startled him, and my next comment
quickly followed. "Have you and your wife ever humbly knelt
down together and prayed for the Lord's guidance?"

"No," was the response to both questions.

"Then, this is my counsel," I said. "Do this, and I promise you
that if you humbly seek divine guidance, you will find strength
and wisdom to overcome any problem before you."

My colleague had never prayed to God. He was not a practicing religious man. In fact, he looked upon organized religion as a sham, a self-righteous profit-making opportunity for money-hungry, charismatic opportunists trying to take advantage of the weak-minded. "Pray?" he said. "Come on, Art, you know I don't pray. I can't kneel down and talk to somebody, or something…," he circled both hands in the air while looking toward the ceiling, "…up there in the heavens. Come on, Art. You know I can't do that."

"Pray," I told him again, "and you will feel a difference. I promise you."

My friend laughed, but even with his denial of divine intervention, he promised he would give it a try; he would kneel and pray to a God he believed didn't even exist. It was the first time such advice had been given to him, and since he had never prayed before, I explained the steps of prayer—how to start, possible questions to ask, and how to close.

I left dinner and went to my hotel room that night with a quiet prayer in my heart that perhaps my colleague might come to a knowledge of God and his Son, Jesus Christ. How could one go through life, I asked myself, denying a supreme being, believing that our very existence lacked divine guidance or intervention?

I recalled the Book of Mormon story of Korihor and the prophet Alma. "Yea, all things denote there is a God," Alma tells the doubting Korihor (Alma 30:44). How true this passage rings today. It appeared that my friend was a modern-day Korihor, denying the very existence of a Creator. Even in observing and admiring the world around him, he failed to accept that any of it was divinely created by a loving God who was aware of his pressing concerns.

A few days after our dinner discussion, I was in New York going over some paperwork when my colleague walked in the door. He said nothing, apparently waiting for me to make the first comment.

"Did you follow my advice?" I asked.

"Not yet," he said. "But I will. I'll give it a try, Art. Just give me some time."

I believed him. He truly wanted to find answers. But because prayer and the thought that someone was actually listening to him was so foreign, it took time to build up the courage and humility to pray.

A couple of weeks went by. I was busy traveling, but I finally ran into him in some forgotten city, where we spent a few private moments. He had a glowing countenance, as if he was excited to tell me something. Indeed he was. "I prayed the other night," he said. "I felt peace. I felt like someone was there…like someone was *listening.*"

What encouraging words to hear. I was thrilled! For him, it was a giant first step, a tremendous leap of faith! To me, it was a man slowly turning his heart to God.

The days turned into weeks, and on occasion I would talk to my colleague about prayer. My friend still didn't have all the answers he was searching for about his relationship and about life, but he was learning—not only from me, but from Heavenly Father. I explained that it would take time, and would require many, many more nights on bended knee and greater faith in his heart. He agreed, and said he would continue, as he put it, "to search for some reason for existence."

As I look back on this experience, I can't help pondering the state of a soul who lacks absolute truth. We live in a world of such uncertainty, ignorance, and confusion that it's no wonder so many are like lost sheep without a shepherd. We must have faith enough to understand one truth: Answers about life can be obtained only from the One who created it. He knows all things, and only he is the unquestioned authority on all that really matters in this world. Seeking wisdom from God through prayer is like asking a music teacher how to read music, a bricklayer how to lay bricks, a carpenter how to work wood. Should we not look to God to ask about life?

Part Five

"Inasmuch as Ye Have Done It unto One of the Least of These My Brethren, Ye Have Done It unto Me" (Matt 25:40)

Our greatest gifts to mankind will not be our possessions, but our kind words, our forgiving hearts, and our genuine compassion.

"Inasmuch as Ye Have Done It unto One of the Least of These My Brethren, Ye Have Done It unto Me"

Foreword

In the early 1980s, while working as a young production assistant and fill-in weekend reporter in Salt Lake City, I had the opportunity of meeting Tom Shell, at the time one of the national networks' most recognized correspondents. He worked for ABC News, and was covering the massive flooding in Utah caused by melting snow. The spring runoff was absolutely amazing; it created rivers of water flowing directly through several mountainside cities and towns, including Salt Lake City. Many of you may remember the scene: a maze of sandbagged aqueducts channeling torrents of water through downtown and elsewhere. It seemed like every stream had turned into a raging river, and every creek bed had become a sizable rush of water.

I accompanied Mr. Shell as he made his way from one location to the next, watching in utter amazement as he witnessed the organization and service rendered by thousands of people, all acting as one in purpose. It was literally one great act of selfless service after another that saved countless neighborhoods, livestock, and even lives. Every time there was a breach in a man-made dike, it was quickly fixed with sandbags donated and placed by many willing hands.

At the end of Mr. Shell's few days in Utah, after he had filed several reports aired throughout the country, I had the opportunity of speaking with him. I was a young, extremely impressionable reporter at the time, so what he said had a profound impact on me. "I've covered dozens of disasters in my life," he said, "but I have never seen unity and brotherhood like this." He was visibly moved by the actions of thousands of flood victims, as well as many others who weren't even affected by the floods, yet helped those in need. "It's scary," he said. "I've seen one man make one phone call, and in less than one hour, 200 residents are building a wall of sandbags around a house to save it. It really is amazing." He was speaking of a stake president making a call to a bishop. I was there; I remember watching the chain of priesthood authority in action and witnessing the awesome result of that one phone call. "I've never witnessed this kind of concern for others," he added. "It's powerful; it really is."

The Prophet Joseph Smith spoke often of such love and service. Indeed, his entire life was centered on lifting, caring, loving and helping those who were spiritually and physically less fortunate. "Love," he said, "is one of the chief characteristics of Deity, and ought to be manifested by those who aspire to be the sons of God. A man filled with the love of God, is not content with blessing his family alone, but ranges through the whole world, anxious to bless the whole human race" (*History of the Church, vol. 4, p. 227).*

In my coverage of events throughout the world, I can recall dozens of examples of people anxious to bless others with their willing hearts, hands, and selfless generosity. But let us not forget the small, simple acts of kindness that also mean so much.

On one occasion, I was watching a high school soccer match. About halfway through the game, one of the players injured his foot and had to be carried off the field. He seemed to be in a great deal of pain, so for the rest of the game he sat on the bench with his leg slightly elevated. Unfortunately, his team lost the contest.

When the match was over, the visiting players, most looking pretty glum in the wake of their loss, walked across the field and headed toward a waiting bus. The boy with the injured foot sat alone on the bench, watching as his teammates began to board the bus. He seemed to be friendless. But one young man looked back and quickly returned. Putting his arm around the injured player, he helped him to the bus. What a sight it was! I silently cheered for the young man, grateful that loving hearts can still be found in today's world.

This helpful young man's name was Matthew. He happened to be a member of the Church, the only Mormon on his soccer team, and one of three members at his 2,000-student high school.

Several days after the game, I telephoned Matthew from my office and told him I was impressed with his show of concern for his teammate. But I wanted to dig a little deeper. "Why did you return to the bench to help the injured player?" I asked. "Why didn't you just continue to follow the crowd and walk to the bus with the rest of the team?"

"I don't know," he replied. "I just saw him sitting there, and I thought he needed some help. There was nothing great about what I did. I just thought the guy needed some help getting to the bus, so I helped him."

Matthew's response was very matter-of-fact. But after giving it some thought, I realized the young man had a valid point. There was nothing particularly "great" about what he'd done—not by the world's definition of the word, anyway. Helping the injured player was a rather simple act that any of the soccer players could have done. The difference was that nobody else did it, and Matthew did.

Willing hearts for so-called "great" challenges are easy to find, because, in the end, there is a sense of accomplishment and perhaps the expectation of praise. Unfortunately, the world's simple and modest challenges to perform service often go ignored. Such opportunities are overlooked every day.

I have always believed that true kindness and compassion are exemplified by those who remember and take advantage of simple opportunities for service in their lives. Helping an injured player off the field may be "nothing great" to Matthew and others, but the Lord looks upon such good deeds very differently. As he said, "If ye have done it unto the least of these my brethren, ye have done it unto me."

When the Prophet Joseph Smith was locked away in Carthage Jail with his brother Hyrum, John Taylor, and Willard Richards, he asked Brother Taylor to sing a song. It was a song most beloved by the Prophet, and, probably very aware of his impending death, he wanted to hear it again and again. The song was "A Poor Wayfaring Man of Grief."

I remember singing this song as a young man, but I never really comprehended the true meaning of it until many years later when I began to listen to the words, understand them, and come to know why the Prophet Joseph enjoyed hearing the lyrics. He had a perfect knowledge of the Savior's love, and he spent his days trying to extend that love to others. It's no wonder that this beautiful hymn was one of his favorites. It is now one of mine.

A poor wayfaring Man of grief Hath often crossed me on my way,
Who sued so humbly for relief That I could never answer nay.
I had not pow'r to ask his name, Where-to he went, or whence he came;
Yet there was something in his eye That won my love; I knew not why.

Once, when my scanty meal was spread, He entered; not a word
he spake,
Just perishing for want of bread. I gave him all; he blessed it, brake,
And ate, but gave me part again. Mine was an angel's portion then,
For while I fed with eager haste, The crust was manna to my taste.

I spied him where a fountain burst Clear from the rock; his
strength was gone.
The heedless water mocked his thirst; He heard it, saw it hurrying on.
I ran and raised the suff'rer up; Thrice from the stream he drained
my cup,
Dipped and returned it running o'er; I drank and never thirsted more.

'Twas night; the floods were out; it blew A winter hurricane aloof.
I heard his voice abroad and flew To bid him welcome to my roof.
I warmed and clothed and cheered my guest And laid him on my
couch to rest;

Then made the earth my bed, and seemed In Eden's garden while I dreamed.

Stript, wounded, beaten nigh to death, I found him by the highway side.
I roused his pulse, brought back his breath, Revived his spirit, and supplied
Wine, oil, refreshment—he was healed. I had myself a wound concealed,
But from that hour forgot the smart, And peace bound up my broken heart

In pris'n I saw him next, condemned To meet a traitor's doom at morn.
The tide of lying tongues I stemmed, And honored him 'mid shame and scorn.
My friendship's utmost zeal to try, He asked if I for him would die.
The flesh was weak; my blood ran chill, But my free spirit cried, "I will!"

Then in a moment to my view The stranger started from disguise.
The tokens in his hands I knew; The Savior stood before mine eyes.
He spake, and my poor name he named, "Of me thou has not been ashamed.
These deeds shall thy memorial be; Fear not, thou didst them unto me."

(Hymns, No. 29)

It is my hope that the stories and experiences in these pages can bring us closer to an understanding of the abundant opportunities life provides to help, serve, and love those around us. By doing so, we can become true disciples of Christ, living more fully his commandment to "love one another" (see John 13:34).

THE GOOD SAMARITAN
Rescue of a Woman in South Central L.A.

One of my favorite stories in the New Testament is the parable of the good Samaritan, which is one of the most familiar parables of the Lord's teachings. I'm sure you have read the scriptural passages many times; even so, one cannot read or hear the verses of this parable enough. Its message is simple but powerful, and too important to ever suggest we have heard the story too many times.

The Savior's parable is preceded by the questioning of "a certain lawyer," who was apparently trying to catch the Lord in a trap. Said the lawyer, "Master, what shall I do to inherit eternal life?" (Luke 10:25)

Jesus knew the man's heart, and was well aware that he prided himself on his great knowledge of the law. The Lord replied with a question of His own: "What is written in the law? How readest thou?" (Luke 10:26)

The lawyer answered by reciting current law: "Thou shall love the Lord thy God with all thy heart, and with all thy soul, and with all thy strength, and with all thy mind; and thy neighbor as thyself" (Luke 10:27). With the boastful, self-righteous disposition of lawyers during this time, and because of the nature of his question, we can readily assume that the lawyer felt quite sure that he, himself, was living the law.

The Master's response was simply, "Thou hast answered right: this do, and thou shalt live" (Luke 10:28).

The lawyer's second question gives readers a clearer understanding of the man's heart, although the Lord was clearly aware of his evil intent: "And who is my neighbor?" (Luke 10:29)

Luke recorded the Lord's response to the question:

> And Jesus answering said, A certain man went down from Jerusalem to Jericho, and fell among

thieves, which stripped him of his raiment, and wounded him, and departed, leaving him half dead.

And by chance there came down a certain priest that way: and when he saw him, he passed by on the other side.

And likewise a Levite, when he was at the place, came and looked on him, and passed by on the other side.

But a certain Samaritan, as he journeyed, came where he was: and when he saw him, he had compassion on him,

And went to him, and bound up his wounds, pouring in oil and wine, and set him on his own beast, and brought him to an inn, and took care of him.

And on the morrow when he departed, he took out two pence, and gave them to the host, and said unto him, Take care of him; and whatsoever thou spendest more, when I come again, I will repay thee (Luke 10:30-34).

I can't read this beautiful parable without being reminded of a story I covered when working at KABC-TV in Los Angeles a number of years ago. The story literally evolved before my eyes, and it had remarkable similarities to this biblical account of the good Samaritan. It was the story of a woman, her family, and their burned-down home.

After I reported to the office early one morning, I was sent to the home of a divorced woman and her three children who lived in a troubled neighborhood of south central Los Angeles. Late the evening before, a group of wild young men had driven by the family's modest home and tossed a molotov cocktail through the front living room window. When the bottle hit the floor, it immediately exploded into a ball of fire. The flames quickly ignited the curtains and furniture, and within minutes the entire room was ablaze.

A woman and her three sons, sleeping in the back bedrooms, were awakened by the crackling sound of fire and the deadly fumes of smoke. The woman, after realizing her home was on fire, jumped out of bed, raced down the hall to rescue her children, and attempted an escape through the living room to the door. The flames, which by now had completely engulfed the front living area, prevented her from using that escape route, so she returned to her bedroom, hoping for a getaway through her window. Not a chance; the windows in the house were covered with burglar bars bolted to the outside wall. The small family was trapped; the flames had already consumed most of the house and were slowly getting closer to the bedroom.

A passerby rushed to the home after noticing the fire. Hearing the screams of the family in the front bedroom, he risked his own life by literally pulling the burglar bars out of the wall sockets. One by one, this stranger helped the children to safety. The last one out was the mother. By the time she escaped the house, she had minor burns on her body and was suffering from smoke inhalation.

Firefighters arrived soon after and tried to extinguish the blaze, but it was too late. The woman and her three children could only watch helplessly as all of their meager possessions went up in smoke. Everything in the house was gone. The only belongings the family had left were the clothes they were wearing, an old broken-down 1962 Chevrolet parked next to the house, and of course, each other. But soon they didn't even have that.

Later in the day, the woman's in-laws arrived at the house. Realizing that she could no longer care for her three young children, the woman consented to having her ex-husband take them. She had a troubled life, and now she had lost everything. Even her most precious possessions, her children, were gone.

When I arrived at the woman's blackened and destroyed home, I found her lying down on the front seat of the old vehicle parked next to the house. She was crying. I knocked on the window of the car to get her attention. "Excuse me, madam," I said. "I'm sorry about the loss of your home." At this point, I wasn't aware that she had lost her children as well. "Perhaps if you talk with us for a moment, we could help with your situation." She agreed.

For the next few minutes, without the camera rolling, this pitiful-looking woman explained to me all that had transpired. Her tearful account touched me. It was difficult to hear of such a tragedy, and yet even more troubling to think that this woman was left friendless. She hadn't received a single offer of help from anyone—not her family, her in-laws, not even those who called her a friend. Her only refuge and miserable comfort was the old vehicle on the side of her burned-down house.

After she explained her desperate plight, I helped her out of the car and we walked into her home. There was literally nothing left but the skeleton frame of the house. Everything inside was burned, blackened, and turned into rubble and ashes. She wept as she looked over what was left of her scanty belongings. She had had very little to begin with, and now she had nothing. Even the clothes on her back were blackened with soot and reeked of smoke.

We interviewed this unfortunate woman as she described in horrifying detail the nightmare she and her children had lived through. The story airing that night on the evening news was a heart-wrenching account of her desperate plight and her plea for help. After the news, the station received dozens of calls from people expressing their desire to assist her. Because she lived in her car and didn't have a phone, the desk assistants were given instructions to give callers the woman's address and explain that they would likely find her inside the old vehicle next to the burned-out home.

By the time I reported to work the next morning, the station had received more than a hundred calls from people willing to help this woman in some way. I suggested that we do a follow-up story to see if any of the callers had actually made good on their promised assistance.

My cameraman and I approached the burned-down house and noticed the woman sitting in the front seat of her parked car. We watched from a distance as several vehicles, obviously not from this impoverished neighborhood, stopped in front of the house.

Sometimes the person in the vehicle would look at the surroundings and then drive off; or a person would emerge, walk by the desperate woman and her house, and get back in their car and leave. Occasionally someone would even approach the vehicle, knock on the window, and appear to be handing the woman some money. There must have been a dozen or so cars that stopped.

After capturing much of this on video, we had begun inching our way closer to the house when we saw another vehicle stop. A middle-aged man got out of the car, walked over to the vehicle, knocked on the window, and began speaking to the woman. We approached the two with the camera rolling to learn more of what they were talking about. About that time, the gentleman was helping the woman out of her car and leading her down the walkway to his own vehicle. I noticed she was still wearing the same torn, smoke-damaged, smelly clothing she had been wearing the day of the fire.

The man threw a light blanket across her shoulders, put one arm around her, helped her get inside his vehicle, then drove off. We followed as they made their way to a roadside inn only a few blocks away. He helped the woman out of the car, again put his arm around her shoulders to comfort her, and led her to the front desk of the inn. "This woman's house was burned down," the man told the innkeeper. "She needs a place to stay and some food to eat."

We watched, and with the camera rolling, recorded this amazing event as it unfolded before our eyes. "Here is money enough for two months' rent," the man said as he handed some bills to the innkeeper. "And here is more money so she can eat."

The woman was nearly in tears. She was beaming at this stranger's generosity, and I was awestruck at his obvious willingness to help.

The man turned to the frail-looking woman, gave her some money to buy clothes, and then gave her what she probably needed most: a hug. "You are not forgotten," he said. "I hope this is enough to take care of yourself until you get things in order."

The moment was beautiful. It absolutely brought the parable of the good Samaritan to life. And what made this event even more memorable as an act of genuine compassion were the words of the gentleman to the innkeeper just before he walked out the door. "Take care of this woman," he said. "I'll return in a couple of months. If I need to pay you more, I will."

It was the Christmas season when this remarkable incident occurred—a time, perhaps, when the entire Christian world is more compassionate, more sensitive, more loving and kind. What I witnessed was truly a gentle act of loving and caring service. But I believe this gentleman would have done the same thing at any other time of year. He set a beautiful example of how we should extend ourselves with genuine love for others.

The story of this good Samaritan aired on the evening news that night, and I subsequently received a great deal of praise for capturing such an incident on video. But the accolades were clearly misdirected. They should have been given to the gentleman who gave viewers a look at true compassion—a man whose selfless desire was only to love this neighbor he never knew, more than he loved himself.

As I drove home that evening, I thought about this incident and how I could respond similarly to those in need. We may not have the opportunity or resources to give as this gentleman did, but I'm confident that every day, in our own little world, we are presented with many opportunities to give of our time, energy, talents, and love. Our service could be as simple as holding a door open, lending encouraging words to someone in need, or perhaps just having an open ear and being a friend. Too often we overlook opportunities to serve, believing there is simply no time in our busy lives to help some unfortunate soul. Still, whatever our circumstances, there are unlimited opportunities to follow the example of the good Samaritan. The challenge is putting aside our selfish desires and turning our hearts toward others.

In the parable of the Samaritan, Jesus used extreme examples to make his point clear. It wasn't the priest or the Levite who helped the wounded Jew; it was the Samaritan—the Jewish people's worst enemy. To make certain the lawyer understood the story, the Lord turned to his original accuser and asked, "Which now of these three, thinkest thou, was neighbour unto him that fell among the thieves?" (Luke 10:36)

Now, the lawyer might well have hesitated in answering the question after realizing that his trap had been turned against him. But the fact that he even responded to the Lord's question indicates that he might have swallowed a little of his pride. So it was that he answered, perhaps with a measure of humility, "He that shewed mercy on him" (Luke 10:37).

"Go, and do thou likewise" (Luke 10:37), the Master commanded.

The Lord's powerful yet tactful way of teaching once again proved flawless. His charge is undeniably clear: Our responsibility is to stretch out our hands and hearts to others, and to lovingly respond to their needs.

His final words to the lawyer are worth repeating as a gentle but firm reminder to us all. "Go, and do thou likewise," the Master said. May we find it in our hearts to listen and obey.

THROUGH THE EYES OF A MISSIONARY
On the Road in North Carolina

A few years ago, I was in a small, run-down little town in North Carolina, covering the racially-charged trial of a former army soldier accused of gunning down a black couple. The soldier was white, and was suspected of leading a small group of white supremacists who had a deep hatred toward Jews and blacks. Participants often spoke of how to "get rid" of those they despised. Each member of the hate group was eventually convicted of murder and sentenced to life in prison. The trial was an ugly, glaring exposé of the secret lives that people often lead.

One thing that added to the depressing nature of this story was the town in which the trial was being held. At the time, I thought of it as a remote, dusty village that lacked character and, even worse, any form of life after eight-thirty in the evening. Unfortunately, that was about the time I would finish filing my evening and morning news reports and start looking for a place to eat. Nearly everything was closed by that time, and I would often find myself at a fast-food restaurant for dinner. Because of the length of the trial, I had to return and cover it on a few occasions, and I found myself really beginning to hate the town.

Late one evening after filing my reports, I was feeling rather tense and impatient as I searched out a place to eat. In my drive down the main street, I was caught behind a slow-moving, beat-up old pickup truck. Angry and frustrated over the driver's lack of skill, I asked myself, *Who would ever want to live in this place? There isn't anything in this town.* I was not in a terribly good mood.

During this moment of not feeling the least bit interested in what this town had to offer, the Lord awakened my senses and reminded me of a missionary who was serving somewhere in North Carolina. The missionary was Elder Craig Mackay, a priest during my days as Young Men's president in California. He had served on the stake youth leadership council; we had become good friends and often spent time together. As I continued my slow progress behind the pickup truck, I called his parents on my cell phone to find out just where Elder Mackay was, and learned to my surprise that he was serving in the same town where the trial was being held. Elder Mackay's parents didn't have their son's phone number, but they did have his address. By now the road had opened up to a couple of lanes. I passed the driver of the truck and made my way to the side of the road to make a few more calls. Using some of my reporter skills, I was able to track down the mission president's number and was given clearance to call and visit my friend.

It was late that same evening, perhaps nine or ten o'clock, when I made my first call to Elder Mackay. The line was busy on the first call. I waited about thirty minutes, then called back. "Hello!" the voice on the other end said. "This is Elder Mackay." Just like a missionary, he sounded unexplainably enthusiastic.

"Elder Mackay!" I responded with the same tone of excitement. "This is Art Rascon. How are you doing?"

He was shocked. The last time I had called him was a year earlier, soon after Hurricane Fran had ravaged the coast of North Carolina and I had been sent to cover the disaster. Before my trip home, I dropped by his apartment and stayed until my flight left the next morning. This time, my call gave him some indication that I might be in the vicinity.

After his more than enthusiastic response, he quickly asked what he clearly wanted to know. "So, Art, are you in town? Tell me you are!" I explained that I was; I'd been in town for a couple of days, covering a trial.

I'll never forget his next comment, which spoke against everything I had said about this little town. It was a frightening contrast. "Hey, Art," he said, "isn't this a great town? Man, I love this place. I love the people here."

My heart sank. I was beginning to feel guilty.

He went on. "This place is so terrific! The people here are so open to the gospel. The Spirit has been working on this town; these people are ready!"

I couldn't believe what I was hearing. I felt like crawling into a hole, but I knew I was being taught a much-needed lesson. Without any prompting from me, he continued with increasing enthusiasm. "Man, Art, I've only been here a couple of months, and it's been tough, but there are some neat people who are ready for baptism!" Then, with the fervor of missionary zeal, he said what we often hear missionaries proclaim: "If my companion and I are here six more months, this town will be translated!"

I laughed. But deep inside, I was crying. Every word he spoke was truth to my ears. I knew this town offered much more than my mortal eyes allowed me to see. My missionary friend was looking through spiritual eyes. Years ago, I had been this young man's teacher; now he was mine. I couldn't help feeling ashamed as he unknowingly taught me about people, about places, about attitudes, and about love. They were lessons I had learned as a youth, and they should have never been forgotten as an adult.

I can clearly remember the counsel of my bishop as I was preparing to serve a mission: "Love the people you serve." Later, when I arrived at the Missionary Training Center, I remember sitting with all the other newly arrived missionaries, listening to the words of MTC President Christiansen. "Love your area, and love the people you serve," he said.

Throughout my adult life, while serving in various callings with the Young Men, I have repeatedly emphasized the importance of serving missions. I have encouraged these prospective missionaries to love the areas to which they are called, and to genuinely love the people they serve. The old saying that "Beauty is in the eye of the beholder" speaks a great deal of truth here.

The eyes of the spiritually awakened will always find the good in people, places, or things. I have learned over time and through vivid experience that there is nothing true love and faith can't conquer. The challenge lies in sharing that love with everyone we meet, and allowing them to feel our genuine love and concern. In doing so, we too can have within us that ever constant missionary zeal and say, "I love this place, and I love the people."

There is a song my lovely wife sings on occasion, and it has become one of my favorites:

> *A child was born in Bethlehem,*
> *Within a cattle stall.*
> *A child whose love was pure enough*
> *To lift and save us all.*
> *He gave His love away,*
> *Gave His life that we might live.*
> *Touched our hearts and souls with*
> *Perfect love,*
> *His love is ours to give.*
> *Give your love away,*
> *There's someone needing you.*
> *Give your love away,*
> *Reach out, in all you do.*
> *For you have His love,*
> *It comes from above,*
> *Give your love away.*
>
> *When life's clock goes ticking by,*
> *The minutes and the years,*
> *Fill your world with happiness,*
> *And wipe away your tears.*
> *Then give your love away,*
> *Share a smile with someone new,*
> *Lend a hand to those who need your love,*
> *And love will return to you.* (Randy and Susan Boothe,
>   composers: Spectrum Music, Spanish Fork, Utah)

May each of us, like my friend Elder Mackay, learn to love, appreciate, and value the people and places in our lives.

MOMENTS OF COMPASSION IN THE MIDST OF ANARCHY
Riots in the City of Angels

I have witnessed some disturbing and graphic forms of domestic violence in my years as a journalist, but few are as dreadfully memorable as the 1992 riots in the city of Los Angeles. In fact, the United States had not seen such a degree of civil disturbance, anarchy, violence, and resulting death since the Civil War. In three days of rioting, more than sixty-five people lost their lives, thousands of buildings were damaged, burned down, or destroyed, and literally tens of thousands of people were blamed for taking part in the rebellion. I was appalled as I watched the horrific scenes before me, guilt-ridden because I could not do more to stop it, and embarrassed that this evil would take place in a supposedly civilized, God-fearing country.

The rapid disintegration of order and morals began on April 29 of that year, in the wake of a lengthy trial of four white officers from the Los Angeles Police Department who had been charged with several counts of assault in connection with the beating of black motorist Rodney King. Surely you recall the video of the beating, played so many times by the television media that it almost became a regular feature on the nightly news.

I was covering the story from the Simi Valley Courthouse, where the trial was being held and where the verdicts were released. It was the moment the nation was waiting for. Networks went to great expense to carry the verdicts "live," and throughout the country people stayed close to their television and radio stations to hear and watch the news. Soon the moment arrived.

One by one the verdicts were read, and one by one the words "not guilty" fell from the bailiff's lips. Within hours, those simple words unleashed a torrent of fury in this city that had prided itself on showing the world a face of multicultural tolerance. But there was little tolerance on this day—only immediate outrage and cries of disapproval from many in the courtroom. The judge quickly silenced the objections by slamming his gavel on the bench and demanding a sense of decorum. Just outside the courthouse the reaction was much the same, but it grew progressively worse and mushroomed into a rage of obscenities that reverberated from one end of the parking lot to the other. Soon the crowd of nearly a hundred turned into an angry mob, chanting, "NO JUSTICE, NO PEACE!"

The courtroom was cleared, and the irate group joined the shouting throng outside the courthouse. One by one, the vindicated officers emerged from the building, surrounded individually by a dozen or so sheriff's deputies who walked in unison with their arms locked, trying to keep the vicious mob from assaulting the officers. The people were in a frenzy as they reached, kicked, hit, spat, and shouted obscenities. It was unlike anything I had ever witnessed; a truly revolting scene.

I was in the middle of the mass of hysteria, trying to get reaction from one of the officers, when the microphone cable got wrapped around someone's foot. The tangle forced me to stop walking, and I was immediately pushed to the ground and trampled underfoot. I couldn't get up until the crowd had passed.

I can't believe this is happening, I told myself. I looked around in a state of disbelief at the rapid decline of order and the indignant behavior of the angry crowds. It was late in the afternoon, but I already knew this was going to be a long night of trouble in the streets. Little did I realize that this was just the beginning of three days of utter chaos. Allow me to share a few excerpts from my journal. (Please forgive the roughness of the writing, as I wasn't expecting it to be widely read.)

4-29-92—Wednesday
> *Was driving home from the courthouse when I heard the first sign of erupting violence. The radio announcer talked about some disturbance at the corner of Florence and Normandie in South Central*

Los Angeles. The assignment desk told me to stand by. I spent a couple of hours at home watching a live broadcast from choppers in the air showing gangs of youth pulling people from their vehicles and throwing rocks and bottles. Was called in later in the evening and sent to South Central L.A. Several people were beaten in the streets tonight. The scene was violent, ugly and saddening. I wasn't witness to all of it. I arrived too late. But when I arrived I heard the stories. Men, women, and even young children are yanked from their vehicles while stopped at traffic lights and beaten senselessly. A woman pleads for help, only to be pelted with more rocks. She is eventually rescued by a passerby and rushed to the hospital. A white man is pulled from his vehicle and kicked, punched, and mobbed by a group of thugs. The group is young but too overpowering for the elderly man. They begin to throw rocks at the man ... he is near death when a black man comes to his rescue. "If you want to kill this man, you'll have to kill me first," he screams. The group of young thugs walks away. What power in his words, what strength in his stature, what an example in the middle of such rebellion. It was the first sign of compassion I've heard of yet. The violence seems to be spreading. There are reports of chaos coming from everywhere. I fear I may be in the middle of it all for some time. There was little sleep tonight. I hope and pray tomorrow will be a day in which goodness overcomes evil.

4-30-92—Thursday

We live in a country that by and large is a Christian nation, one that proclaims a great love of the Lord and obedience to his laws. I have witnessed precious little of that today. I can't believe what I have seen. It's really scary to think that in only a matter of one day, a society could turn so ugly and violent. There is complete anarchy and lawlessness. Everywhere around me, crime and a mob mentality are running rampant. There are not hundreds in the streets, or even thousands; there are tens of thousands taking part in the pillaging of a city. People are running wild; they are burning, looting, destroying, plundering, and dismantling everything in their path.

What has happened to common sense? What has happened to reason? To conscience? To the light of Christ? These people know they are doing wrong. How can they think otherwise? The light of Christ is in them, as it is in everyone… only they have chosen to ignore it.

Reports of many deaths are coming in. I have seen many businesses burned… don't know if anyone was inside. I have heard too many gunshots to number. They echo throughout the city like sirens. Police officers stand on some street corners with their hands holding fast to their pistols. But all they do is watch. They are overpowered. Every cop must be outnumbered 300 to one. I learned how quickly seemingly good people can turn on you when mob mentality sets in. I was with my cameraman on a street corner, watching a large group of people tearing apart a shopping strip. The electronics store was a popular site… it was the first to be looted, ripped apart, and burned. The group made their way down the strip. They noticed us and started yelling and screaming while pointing fingers. I knew they were angry—it was in their eyes. In the middle of their plunder of the strip, they turned on us… all at once. My cameraman and I quickly looked at each other and shouted in unison, "RUN!" I had to keep a slower pace because my partner was lugging the camera. The group was quickly approaching. It didn't take them long to reach us. They were young, fast, and angry. We had equipment to haul. They were on us, and started swinging their hands and kicking their feet. My photographer was hit from behind and dropped to the ground. I stumbled to help him get up and was hit from behind as well. The camera was in pieces; we ignored it and ran for our lives. We must have run nearly a block before jumping in our vehicle and speeding off. The mob continued to chase us, throwing rocks, bottles, and anything they could find.

We returned to Hollywood and the ABC studios. After relaying our experience, my cameraman was given another camera and we were told to get back on the streets to continue coverage of the story. Executives explained they were trying to find bulletproof vests, or at least supply us with bodyguards. I returned to the city and said a silent prayer, thanking the Lord that we had survived the attack, and asking for his continued protection. I felt as though the Lord was listening. I learned that others were praying for my safety. Patti told me of this late tonight. She paged me, wondering how I was doing. She wasn't aware of the eruption of lawlessness until she received several calls from members of our home ward and other concerned neighbors and friends. It was amazing. "I just wanted you to know, Patti, that we are praying for your husband and hope the Lord will protect him," they said. After a few such calls, she contacted me directly. I thank the Lord for the kindness and thoughtfulness of so many who went out of their way to pray for my safety and to comfort my family. Their prayers undoubtedly helped me live.

5-1-92—Friday

Last night was an eerie scene. The city was dark, except for fires that dotted the landscape. Power was

out to most of the city, and the streets were clear of vehicles. Most roads throughout South Central and elsewhere were closed. The city stood still most of the night, but fires continued to burn. I had little sleep, except for an hour or two in the vehicle. We kept busy racing from street corner to street corner. I am amazed at the level of chaos and blatant disregard for human life and property. It's shocking how quickly a seemingly law-abiding citizenry can explode into a demonic throng of selfish scoundrels. Isn't this country, the promised land, supposed to be the world leader and example of how a civilized and democratic nation should act? Instead, we are the epitome of third-world civil conflict, where murder, plunder in the streets, arson, theft, and complete disorder are commonplace.

Earlier today, I witnessed a telling signal of that lack of compassion and disregard for others. I stood at the corner of a busy intersection, taking a panoramic view of all that was around me. On one corner, a supermarket was being looted, then burned. On another corner, an entire shopping strip was on fire, with flames shooting 40 feet in the air. There were no firefighters in sight. I was standing in front of a large shoe store, still smoldering from a fire that destroyed it last night, and across the street was a dry cleaning shop. It was untouched. What a miracle! The massive glass windows that reached from ceiling to ground were unbroken. I watched as people began walking the perimeter of the store, looking inside, waiting for someone to make the first move. Soon one person grabbed a large brick and tossed it through the window. All it took was one person for hundreds to follow. The shop was soon filled with dozens of people who pillaged the place and began looting it of cash and clothes. While this was occurring, an old vehicle drove to the front of the shop. An elderly woman and her husband jumped out and started yelling at the crowd to stop. "Please," the woman said, "this is my store. Leave it alone!" The crowd ignored her. She spoke louder and tried to grab some of her belongings from another person's arms. "Please leave the clothes alone," she cried louder. They pushed her aside, hard enough for her to land on the ground. From her knees she begged the swarm of rioters to stop. I saw her begin to weep. I wanted to help but couldn't. She clasped her hands together while on her knees and pleaded with the mob. "Please put the clothes back," she cried. "Stop!" The crowd ignored this poor weeping soul, and this time pushed her so that she lost her balance from her knees and fell to the ground. She lay there crying while her husband grabbed a stick to try and stop the thugs. They overpowered him and whipped him a couple of times. He returned to the side of his wife, comforted her, and watched as their business was destroyed. There was no mercy, no compassion, no sense of brotherly love. Do we really live in a society where even basic morals of decency are lost? What a sad, pitiful scene this was. This story not only speaks of the lack of compassion, but of the power of peer pressure. Like lost sheep desperately searching for a shepherd to lead them, this unruly crowd waited for a leader to toss a brick through a window; they waited for the first person to grab a handful of clothes, push aside the desperate woman, and beat the man with a stick. This all seemed to happen so quickly. Too quickly. I understand more clearly now how a people, a society, a nation, can dwindle in unbelief and wickedness so rapidly. Of the hundreds of thousands that live in and around the riot-affected areas, a good number of them decided to join in the criminal activity. "Why are you doing this?" I asked several people carrying out store possessions. "Because everyone else is," was their feeble, narrow-minded response. It's no wonder the violence only escalated with each passing hour.

5-2-92—Saturday

Last night brought another rash of fires and looting. Most of the city was quiet. A strict curfew is now in place. I was actually able to return home for a couple of hours to get some sleep. What a contrast from the war-torn streets of Los Angeles! Although it was in the middle of the night and everyone was asleep, I could still feel of the love, peace, safety, and refuge that our home provided. I felt the comfort of the Spirit and the assurance of my family's love. How could one ever desire anything else?

I slept from about 1:00 a.m. to 3:00 a.m. I didn't want to leave home and head back to the city…back to chaos, confusion, and so much despair…but I had to. I remember driving over the hill and looking upon Los Angeles. A thick smoke filled the sky. As if this city's pollution isn't bad enough. Power was still out in most areas, and fires lit the night sky. At daybreak, the evil that still lingered here awakened, and the masses of people returned to the streets. There was some sense of hope, however. National Guard troops arrived—7,000 of them. They came in choppers, in Humvees, in tanks, and in hundreds of army jeeps. The city was suddenly under military control. Soldiers with M-16 machine guns and flak jackets replaced the overweight rent-a-cops. Troops patrolled the streets as if they had won a great victory. What a sight this was…and in many ways, a great relief. The city was at least partly under control. There were still some fires being set, and hordes of people were still able to rob and pillage some stores. Perhaps the Lord's day, tomorrow, will have a more calming impact on this wild and undisciplined mass of cowards.

5-3-92—Sunday

Got a few hours of rest last night. The most since this violent episode began. I had no desire to return to the city today, but knew I must. This is the Lord's day. A day of peace and rest. In this city of angels, people seemed to turn their hearts back to God. I don't quite understand it all. Church pews everywhere were full. People of all faiths prayed for calm, for peace, for tranquility, for an end to the riotous devastation. How could this be? I thought. Weren't these the same people who only yesterday and the previous two days spent their time destroying the city? I moved from church house to church house in the inner city, but found little comfort from any words that were spoken from the pulpits.

As this city returns to normalcy, I can't help but reflect on the past few days... at how such wickedness could sweep across the land in an outwardly sadistic way. What shocked me the most was not the gangs of youth taking part, but the adults—they easily outnumbered the adolescents. And many of them held their young children by the hand as they raced from store to store, loading their vehicles with stolen goods. Could those with a sure knowledge of truth take part in such mutiny? I would hope they were not among the rioters.

The gospel brings such sureness, such a powerful degree of comfort and encouragement to live righteously, that one has little or no desire to do evil. The Book of Mormon speaks of this. After King Benjamin speaks to his people, they tell him that the Lord has wrought a "mighty change in their hearts." The change was so great "that we have no more disposition to do evil, but to do good continually" (Mosiah 5:2). On this Sabbath day, considering the events of the week, this scripture has more profound meaning. I have witnessed and learned much the past few days. I hope and pray I will never forget the lessons... and will in some way be able to instill in the minds of everyone, including myself, the great need to do more—to live more compassionately, more lovingly, more thoughtfully, and more religiously. By doing so, we follow the Master's footsteps instead of the lost souls who run wild in the streets.

A BOY IN THE LOCKER
Trapped and Forgotten

I don't remember much of my middle and high school education. Those years were rather uneventful, to say the least. Although I always considered myself extremely motivated, persistent, and outgoing, I never involved myself in any sports, activity clubs, debate teams, theater groups, or student organizations. In fact, I can't recall ever attending school dances, parties, sporting events, or dramatic productions. I probably wouldn't be too far from the truth if I said that my peers likely considered me an absolute outcast in school—someone who simply wandered through those red brick tombs, taking up space in hallways, classrooms, and, in a bizarre way, lockers.

Perhaps my low profile at school, however deliberate it was, was the reason I rarely appeared in yearbooks. At the end of every year, along with the rest of the student body, I would anxiously flip through the pages, searching for those candid, silly photographs that captured the so-called "fun times" at school. I never found myself in those pictures. In fact, sometimes I wasn't even found in the more formal settings of individual photographs. On a couple of occasions, after not finding my picture, I remember turning to the back of the yearbook and looking under the heading, "STUDENTS NOT PICTURED." My name wasn't on that list, either. I sometimes wondered if school administrators even knew I was a student at their school.

In light of my laughable middle and high school history, it wasn't much of a surprise when I got caught up in one of the most embarrassing, truly demoralizing experiences of my life. This story, as wild as it might sound, is true—every bit of it. I can vividly remember most of the details of the incident because it had such a profound impact on me.

I was attending school at Bell Junior High in Golden, Colorado. I must have been in the eighth or ninth grade. I had a few friends— not any who I would consider extremely close, but they at least made me feel like I was not completely isolated. Until, of course, they turned on me, stuffed me in a locker, and left me friendless.

Between classes, students were given a few minutes to walk from one class to the next. I was with my usual small group of friends, talking about whatever fourteen- and fifteen-year-olds talk about, and playing with an open, unoccupied locker. The lockers were rather large, maybe four feet high, a foot or so deep, and the same in width. One of my friends would get in the locker, someone would shut it, then we would swing it open. It was a dumb thing to do; but then, we did plenty of dumb things in those days.

Even though I considered myself claustrophobic, I garnered up enough nerve to climb inside the locker. The door was slammed and then quickly opened, and I didn't hesitate to jump out. It was an extremely tight fit and pretty uncomfortable, so I wasn't anxious to try it again, even with my friends egging me on. Besides, the bell had just echoed through the empty halls of the school, and I was already tardy for my next class. Still, my friends kept pressuring me to climb in the locker, "just one more time." I was pretty gullible at that age, so, believing they would keep their promise and quickly let me out, I squeezed myself back into the locker "just one more time." It was a decision I quickly regretted.

"Okay, guys, open the door," I said. They didn't. I heard only the rumbling of laughter and the faint voices of those plotting against me. I tried pressing against the door with my knees and arms, but it didn't do much good. I was boxed in too tightly to allow much movement.

"Let me out, guys!" I yelled a bit louder. There was no audible response, just laughter. I tried in vain to wiggle the handle from the inside, but that didn't work either. My so-called "friends" were holding firmly to the outside handle, and I could feel the pressure of a body against the door. I began to fall into a minor panic. "Get me out of here! Come on guys, let me out!" Again nothing, only laughter and the sounds of several unintelligible voices.

The next thing I heard terrified me so completely that to this day it still rings in my ears. "Get a padlock," I heard someone scream. "Hurry, get a lock!"

My heart sank. I hated tight places, and I was already frantic. I tried to bang on the door with my hands and feet, but there was so little room to move that the sounds were more like thumps instead of loud slams. I yelled again. "Please, guys, let me out! Get me out of here!!" I heard them fiddling with a lock. As I pleaded with them to stop and let me out, I could hear the large, heavy padlock slip through the hole of the locker handle.

"Lock it!" someone screamed. And another voice: "Come on, hurry and lock it."

I yelled louder, knowing it would be my last chance to convince them to rescue me from their malicious scheme. "Don't do it, guys! Come on, please open the door!" I began to cry and plead again. "Open the door, guys! *Open it!*"

My screams were in vain. I heard the padlock snap shut, and the laughter and footsteps of my friends faded into the distance as they made their escape. Their deed was done, their plot successful, their mission accomplished, and their desertion conspiracy complete.

It was deathly quiet, with not even a faint sound of anyone, anywhere. I was alone, abandoned by those who I thought were my closest friends. In fact, they were my *only* friends. Surely this was just a temporary joke, I told myself, and soon enough I would hear them return, open the padlock, and deliver me from this bondage. It never happened; I was left to fend for myself. *How could they do this to me?* I thought. What had I ever done that would lead them to imprison me in a locker? Who would ever concoct this devilish scheme? Never before had I felt so abandoned and forsaken.

To help you envision my surroundings, the locker I was trapped in was located in the middle of a long hallway of lockers, and at both ends of the hallway were stairs leading to a second level. I don't remember any classrooms nearby. Perhaps that's why my screams and pounding against the locker door were not heard.

"Someone help me!" I yelled again and again. "I'm in a locker. Help! Help!" I slipped into a deeper panic. I banged and punched, pounded and kicked, pushed and yelled, but no one responded. I was nestled so firmly inside my tightly closed cocoon that I couldn't leverage myself well enough to exert much strength. I can remember pushing so hard with my feet and hands that I was literally dripping with sweat. The lower and upper portions of the locker were even slightly bent from the pressure of my hands and feet. After a while, I was so exhausted that I allowed my body to go limp. The small metal cage surrounding me was snug enough to prevent me from collapsing.

It was during this time of inactivity that I did something I should have done long before. I said a prayer. "Please help me stay calm," I pleaded with the Lord. "And help me get out of this locker."

From the moment of that prayer, I stopped having the claustrophobic sensations that were racing through my body and sending me into periods of panic. Instead, a sense of peace came over me, a calming spirit that allowed me to come to my senses and realize that although I was deserted by my friends, I was still loved by those who truly mattered, Heavenly Father and Jesus Christ.

Even though I now felt more positive about the situation, I would still bang on the locker every few minutes and yell out loud, hoping that someone would eventually hear me. "Help! Someone help me!" I would suddenly blurt out. I repeated this several times over a period of thirty to forty minutes. Finally, from a distance, there was a faint response.

"Hello," a voice called. "Who's calling? Where are you?" It didn't sound like a student, and I was already growing embarrassed over the possibility that it might be one of the school administrators.

"I'm in a locker," I yelled. "Over here. Help!"

I heard the pounding of feet draw closer. Soon it was obvious that my rescuer was right in front of me. I heard him breathing. I heard his subdued laughter. "How did you ever get inside this locker?" he asked.

"My friends locked me in," I said.

He introduced himself as one of the school janitors. "This is a combination lock. We're going to have to get a saw to cut it off," he said. He left and returned with a hacksaw in a matter of minutes.

The sawing seemed to last an eternity. I could hear the screech of each swing of the blade. My anxiety was almost unbearable; I began to feel emotional and couldn't prevent the tears from welling up and a lump from rising in my throat. Then I heard the school bell ring. It was the signal for the entire student body to change class periods. *How can this be?* I thought. *Have I really been inside this locker for nearly an hour?*

The vibrating noise of the metal saw slowly took second stage to the ever-increasing noise of students shuffling through the hallway. The commotion grew louder, and it was obvious that a crowd was gathering around the janitor. "What's going on?" I heard a student ask.

"I don't know," said another.

"Hey, janitor, what are you doing?" someone else asked. I kept quiet, but feared the janitor's response. Would he let the secret out? I had pleaded, waited, and hoped for my release; now I was dreading it. Perhaps the janitor would ignore the students, the tardy bell would ring, and I would be let out with only my rescuer to face. But it didn't happen that way. Nothing seemed to be happening my way on this day.

"There's a boy in the locker," the janitor blurted out almost proudly. "He's been stuck in here for some time."

Have you ever seen fire follow a stream of gasoline? How about the scream of a child after he stumbles and falls? The word spread faster than that. I couldn't see it happen, but I heard it. It was as clear as a wild throng of students yelling at a football game.

"There's a kid in the locker!" a student yelled, laughing as he said it.

"A kid in the locker?" someone else chimed in. "Hey, guys, there's a boy in the locker!"

The rumbling of "the boy in the locker" reverberated throughout the school. The news was too big for anyone to ignore.

Would this be an event you would want to miss? I could hear the escalating pandemonium beyond the thin piece of sheet metal that separated me from my peers. My only hope was that the tardy bell would ring and administrators would usher everyone to class. But again, it didn't happen that way.

"Who's in the locker, anyway?" a student questioned, followed by another, then another.

"Don't know," said the janitor repeatedly. It was an edge-of-the-seat suspense thriller for the students and the janitor as well. It was obvious the student body was in an uproar just anticipating the grand opening of the locker.

I couldn't believe what was happening. It was too much for me. I was already teary-eyed, but now I began to cry. The stress of being locked up, exhausted, claustrophobic, and on the verge of being released in plain view of the entire student body was more than I could bear. I tried to keep my emotion quiet. In fact, I remember thinking, *This is crazy. I can't let everyone see me crying. I've got to stop crying before I'm let out.*

"Almost finished," the janitor said. "Just about got it. Just a few saws more."

I can't wait, I sarcastically told myself as I visualized my future.

"All right, got it. All done!" the janitor said triumphantly.

He was finally finished. I only wished it had been ten minutes earlier, or later. I heard the lock drop and the handle lift. The door swung open. I was set free, but like a frightened bird just learning to fly, I didn't want to leave my cage.

Seconds passed and I finally stepped out. There I stood, with tears streaming down my face, looking at my peers. The entire student body of my school was laughing and pointing fingers.

I looked around for someone to talk to, someone to seek comfort from, someone to lean on. There was no one. Everyone just stared at me, many of them laughing in mockery and pointing as though I was some strange creature who had just escaped from a dark cave. I covered my face with my hands and slowly walked toward the door that led outside.

My traumatic and humiliating experience was finally over… or had it just begun? The event had such an impact on me and on the students at our school that from then on I was known as "the boy in the locker."

I have long since overcome my claustrophobia, but I can't help recalling the locker experience every time I'm in a tightly enclosed space. Tragically, even more memorable was the isolation and loneliness that I couldn't help feeling, as well as the deep sense of abandonment. I had never before felt so deserted or forsaken. The desertion was most evident when I finally exited the locker. During the moment of my greatest need, I was neglected and cast out, forgotten and ignored. How good it would have felt to have someone approach me and express their concern. What a difference any sympathetic and compassionate act, however small, would have made.

I share this experience, not because I'm wallowing in self-pity, but in hopes that we might all learn from it. Each of us, at some time or another, may find ourselves imprisoned in our own "lockers" of life. Everyone faces periods of adversity during which there is need of a loving, helpful hand from another. I'm certain we have all found ourselves in situations where we feel neglected, where true compassion and genuine sympathy are hard to find. What a difference a gentle touch or a friendly word would make.

I have told this story many times to various youth groups across the country. Recently I received a letter from Nathan Stephens, a young man I grew close to when I was serving as a stake Young Men's president in Thousand Oaks, California. He was serving a mission in Paraguay, where he was learning about love, compassion, service, and sharing his time and talents with others. I had related to him my "boy in the locker" story during a youth gathering several years earlier, when he was barely fourteen years old. He, like others in the group, laughed at my predicament and couldn't believe I would be dumb enough to get inside the locker.

I thought my lesson about the need for compassion had never sunk in. I was wrong. At the end of this beautiful letter from Elder

Stephens was a "PS." It read: "Art, I have learned much on my mission. I would have opened the locker for you, and I wouldn't have been one of those laughing and pointing fingers. I would have tried to help."

May we all be quick to open the lonely, terrifying "lockers" of life for those in need, replacing fear and uncertainty with love, light, and hope. In doing so, we become trusted and beloved disciples of the Master.

CONCLUDING THOUGHTS

One Christmas morning, I opened a rather interesting gift from a dear friend. It was a 9- by 13-inch glass-framed print that portrayed a satirical look at the life of a journalist. At the top of the print was a headline: "Why I Love Being a REPORTER." Beneath it, a series of cartoons depicted reporters as uncaring, egotistical, selfish, sadistic, and otherwise thoughtless individuals who were more concerned about making the front page or the lead story in a newscast than they were about the lives of others. The print gave a rather pitiful image of reporters, but in sad reality, the depiction probably supported many of the public's views about television and print journalists.

My wife and I laughed over some of the scenes, and I called my friend to thank him for the gift (and for his rather warped sense of humor). He was quick to assure me that his gift wasn't meant as a personal jab, and he didn't consider me among the pack of "other reporters." I thanked him for his kindness and wished him a merry Christmas.

A few days after this conversation, I found myself reflecting on this gift from my friend. I had been paged early that morning and told about a "breaking news" story in a remote area of Tennessee. I immediately called the New York assignment desk to get more details. "Art," a calm, seasoned voice said on the other end, "there are some powerful storms moving through Tennessee. A major river has flooded its banks and is wiping out riverbank communities."

"How many are dead or missing?" I asked in a dispassionate tone, as though I had been through this drill a hundred times. "How widespread is the damage, and is the flooding still going on?"

"Well," he said, "we weren't going to send you on this story, but the number of dead has climbed to at least six, and there may be several more missing. We've chartered a jet; it'll be ready to leave within the hour. Give us a call when you get there." An hour later,

I was flying at 40,000 feet from Miami to the small town of Elizabethton, Tennessee. When I arrived, search and rescue teams were still battling high waters and swift currents, desperately trying to reach those perched on tops of trees, and searching for those swallowed up in the raging torrent.

Two days later, when I left the rolling hills of Tennessee, the death toll from flooding had climbed to more than a dozen, and the torrential currents had destroyed hundreds of homes along the riverbank. This was a sad, tragic disaster that left many residents destitute and hopeless. In a matter of hours, the lives of thousands of individuals had been drastically altered. Many had died, and countless properties had been destroyed. Families were separated, and a sense of confusion reigned everywhere. The story was prominently featured on the CBS national evening and morning news programs for two days; but after that, interest in the story quickly faded, and I was told to return to my Miami office.

As I sat in my comfortable seat on the jet ride home, eating my warm chicken sandwich and cold cheesecake, I couldn't help thinking what an unpleasant business this sometimes is. Like the cartoon on the print from my friend, reporters chase after scenes of disaster and misfortune, then profit from them by filling papers and television screens with stories and images. When they have completed their work, they simply walk away from the troubles they have reported and return to the comfort of their homes and offices.

For this reporter, leaving the scene of calamity and destruction is perhaps one of the most difficult things to do. There is always a part of me that wants to stay, help, and witness the conclusion of the real stories behind those that were broadcast. These are the compelling stories that never reach the silver screen, but that clearly have greater eternal meaning. I want to see what becomes of the young man whose deep faith in God helped him live during the days after his parents' tragic death. I want to sit with, listen to, and learn from the nine-year-old victim of a drive-by shooting, dying in his hospital bed, as he shares his final words of love for family and friends. I yearn to be a part of the grim search for a father who has been kidnapped and held somewhere in the jungles of Colombia, while his family learns the true meaning of prayer. I wish to comfort grieving families standing along the shores of Haiti, staring seaward after a capsized ferry has swallowed their loves ones. They know so little about life after death, and have so many unanswered questions.

My greatest hope, in writing this book, is that I have opened your eyes to a new world of journalism. It's a world you rarely see on the evening news—a world where so many search for so much, and in their own quiet and personal way long for greater peace, understanding, and happiness. These desirable and coveted elements of life are not always easy to find, especially in a world filled with ignorance, confusion, and stumbling blocks of uncertainty. But they do exist.

I have never covered a story where I didn't believe the gospel would have helped the person or people involved. In my years of covering a wide variety of events, disasters, personal tragedies, widespread tyranny, and courtroom dramas, one overwhelming question always surfaces: *Why?* In most cases, the question could be succinctly and beautifully answered through knowledge of and faith in our Lord and Savior, Jesus Christ, his restored gospel, and the teachings of modern-day prophets. What a tremendous void there is without such knowledge! Permit me to end this work with one final story to illustrate my point.

Some time ago, I was sent to a small town in rural northern Georgia that had been hard-hit by a powerful tornado, with winds clocked at over 225 miles per hour. The scene was awful, and the path of destruction one of the worst I had ever covered. In many areas, the only evidence that a neighborhood of homes had existed was a row of concrete foundations. The fact that fewer than two dozen people died was a miracle.

As I walked down a small, dusty road, gazing in awe at the flattened trees, downed power lines, scattered debris, and complete destruction, I noticed one home in the midst of the rubble that was hardly touched. It caught me by surprise because it was so obvious. During my coverage of other storms, I had sometimes seen half a street destroyed while the other half was left standing. But this one was different. It seemed that nearly every home around this house was damaged or destroyed. The building stood as a beacon of life at the epicenter of death and destruction. I later learned the story behind the little house that would not fall.

Early that morning, before the tornado hit, the father of the house had gathered his family, all members of the Church, for morning prayer. As they knelt in humble reverence at six-thirty a.m., the father pleaded with his Heavenly Father for a blessing of protection upon his three children, his wife, and their home. After their prayer, when they had scarcely stood up, they heard the thunderous noise of an approaching storm. As the torrential rain and wind grew progressively worse, they rushed to one corner of their home and huddled together for protection.

Within seconds, the wind came whipping through in a monstrous roar. Glass began to crash around them, and through the open windows they could see debris flying everywhere. As they listened to the awful sounds of breaking trees and crushing wood, they felt the pressure of a wind tunnel through their house and sensed the ruination around them. When the tornado finally passed, it was deathly quiet. The family arose from the corner and slowly maneuvered around the shattered glass and fallen debris in their living room to get to the front door. When the family opened the door and glanced around at what had once been their neighborhood, tears came to their eyes as they realized how blessed they were. Their home, although damaged, was the only one standing. Their neighborhood had been literally ripped to shreds, and sadly, five of their neighbors had been killed by the storm.

The anchor of support for this family during their time of great loss was a deep faith in God and in the gospel. They understood the plan of salvation and the purpose of life, and they had come to understand how sacrifice and overcoming adversity could bring forth the blessings of heaven. This family became the "iron rod" that many in the community leaned on for help and comfort when the inevitable question surfaced: Why?

Allow me to contrast this story with another that I covered later that day. As I was making my way through the rubble in search of someone to talk to, I noticed a woman who was holding tightly to a small doll. She stood in the middle of a wasteland of twisted metal, shattered tree limbs, broken pieces of furniture, and other household belongings. She appeared teary-eyed and somewhat emotional. I approached the woman and spoke with her. "Are you searching for something in particular?" I asked.

"Yes," she said tearfully, "just anything. Anything that looks like it's worth saving." She reached down and picked up a soggy stuffed animal with a pull-string attached to it. She yanked the string to see if it worked. The chime began to play, "Twinkle, Twinkle, Little Star."

"Who does the toy belong to?" I asked, hoping she would not tell me of a child who was killed in the tornado.

"It's my four-year-old daughter's," she said. "She's at my parents' house right now. She got a few scrapes and bruises, but she's doing fine." I was relieved.

"Do you remember what happened?" I asked. "Could you tell me where you were when the storm hit?"

She began to get emotional. "I was in bed, and I heard something coming. I ran and grabbed my daughter and just hung on to her as tight as I could. The next thing I knew, I found myself way over there." She pointed to a tree about seventy-five yards from where her mobile home had once stood. "I don't know how I survived," she said. "I just thank God I did."

"What do you attribute your survival to?" I asked, curious as to what she would say.

She paused and looked around at the splintered wreck of her home. "I guess faith in God," she said. "Faith in God helped me live." She continued, but with a puzzled look on her face. "This type of experience makes you think about life. It makes you wonder what it's all for. It makes you think about death, and question whether there really is life after death." Her response made it obvious that this tragedy had triggered a real introspection in her life. "I have so many questions now about everything," she said.

Moments later, as I left this woman, I couldn't help thinking of how the gospel could fill the great void in her life. She was divorced, a single mother, and hungry for answers to life's most pressing questions. As I thought of her, then considered the LDS family I had learned of earlier in the day, the contrast was clearly evident. One had a sure knowledge of where greater peace, understanding, and happiness could be found. The other was still searching.

As I continued my walk down the dusty road and away from the tornado's swath of destruction, I noticed a large throng of young men wearing rough clothes. They were ready for some serious work. "Where are you guys from?" I asked.

"We're missionaries from the Mormon Church," one young man blurted out in a strong, bold voice.

"There are 200 of us, and we're here to help clean up this mess," another said.

"There's a woman over there," I said, gesturing to the lady I had just spoken to. "She needs your help cleaning—and even more help with answering questions about life."

"Great!" they said.

The group hurried along like energetic children running to a playground. I watched them work for a while, amazed at their enthusiasm and envious of their circumstances. Like angels from heaven, they had come to do more than clean up piles of debris. They had also come to purify hearts and souls, and to bring those searching for a shepherd the peace, understanding, and happiness they were yearning for.

This is why I love being a reporter, I thought. *To witness people change their lives, grow in faith, and understand the wisdom of God's plan.*

There is no greater light than the one shared by those who truly seek to know God's laws and live them. Such knowledge provides answers to today's most difficult questions, and those answers can lead us to great happiness. Each story I encounter teaches me something about life, death, people, places, things—and about how a person can better prepare for what lies ahead: eternity.

As Latter-day Saints, we believe the underlying gospel principle that brings us closer to God and to his restored truths is faith. It's faith in a God who really does exist. Faith that we are his children and he loves us. Faith in his Son, Jesus Christ, and in his glorious resurrection. Faith that God's church exists today, with Jesus Christ as its cornerstone. Faith in modern-day revelation and a living prophet. And faith that we can one day return to our Heavenly Father if we accept and live the teachings of the gospel. What greater reason is there to live as we should, and to share this important, life-changing message with others along the way?

I pray that this work will in some way help us to that end.